ALSO BY ANDREW BACEVICH

Breach of Trust:
How Americans Failed Their Soldiers and Their Country

Washington Rules:
America's Path to Permanent War

The Limits of Power:
The End of American Exceptionalism

The Long War:
A New History of U.S. National Security Policy Since World War II

The New American Militarism:
How Americans Are Seduced by War

American Empire:
The Realities and Consequences of U.S. Diplomacy

The Imperial Tense:
Prospects and Problems of American Empire

THE AGE OF ILLUSIONS

THE AGE
OF
ILLUSIONS

HOW AMERICA SQUANDERED
ITS COLD WAR VICTORY

ANDREW J. BACEVICH

METROPOLITAN BOOKS

HENRY HOLT AND COMPANY   NEW YORK

Metropolitan Books
Henry Holt and Company, LLC
Publishers since 1866
120 Broadway
New York, NY 10271
www.henryholt.com

Metropolitan Books® and ® are registered trademarks of
Henry Holt and Company, LLC.

Library of Congress Cataloging-in-Publication Data

Names: Bacevich, Andrew J., author.
Title: The age of illusions : How America Squandered Its Cold War Victory /
    Andrew J. Bacevich.
Description: First edition. | New York : Metropolitan Books, Henry Holt and
    Company, 2020. | Includes bibliographical references and index.
Identifiers: LCCN 2019007089 | ISBN 9781250175083 (hardcover)
Subjects: LCSH: United States—Politics and government—1989– | Cold
    War—Influence. | Executive power—United States—History. | Hegemony—
    United States—History. | United States—Social conditions—1980– |
    United States—History—1969–
Classification: LCC E839.5 .B33 2019 | DDC 352.23/50973—dc23
LC record available at https://lccn.loc.gov/2019007089

ISBN: 978-1-250-17508-3

Our books may be purchased in bulk for promotional, educational, or business use.
Please contact your local bookseller or the Macmillan Corporate and Premium
Sales Department at (800) 221-7945, extension 5442, or by email at
MacmillanSpecialMarkets@macmillan.com.

First Edition 2020

Designed by Kelly S. Too

Printed in the United States of America

1 3 5 7 9 10 8 6 4 2

To Eliot A. Cohen,
with admiration, affection, and enduring gratitude

In America, though, life seems to move faster than anywhere else on the globe and each generation is promised more than it will get: which creates, in each generation, a furious bewildered rage, the rage of people who cannot find solid ground beneath their feet.

James Baldwin, *Notes of a Native Son*

CONTENTS

THE AGE OF ILLUSIONS

INTRODUCTION

"Without the Cold War, what's the point of being an American?"[1]

Harry "Rabbit" Angstrom, novelist John Updike's late-twentieth-century Everyman, posed that question just as the "long twilight struggle" was winding down. More than a quarter of a century later, Rabbit's plaintive query still awaits a definitive answer. Indeed, the passage of time has only sown confusion about whether there is a point to being an American.

Even as the Cold War was ending, Updike's surrogate was not alone in feeling at a loss. By the 1980s, the Cold War had become more than a mere situation or circumstance. It was a state of mind. As had Rabbit, most Americans had come to take its existence for granted. Like the polar ice cap or baseball's status as the national pastime, it had acquired an appearance of permanence. So its passing caught Rabbit's fellow citizens unawares. Those charged with managing the Cold War were, if anything, even more surprised. The enterprise to which they had devoted their professional lives had suddenly vanished. Here was a contingency that the sprawling U.S.

national security apparatus, itself a product of the anti-Communist crusade, had failed to anticipate.

At one level, of course, the surprise could not have been more gratifying. In the epic competition pitting West against East, the God-fearing against the godless, and democracy against totalitarianism, "our side" had won. All-out nuclear war had been averted. The cause of freedom, which Americans felt certain they themselves embodied, had prevailed. Victory was decisive, sweeping, and unequivocal.

In another sense, however, the passing of the Cold War could not have been more disorienting. In 1987, a senior adviser to Soviet leader Mikhail Gorbachev had warned, "We are going to do a terrible thing to you—we are going to deprive you of an enemy."[2] As the Soviet Union passed out of existence, Americans were left not just without that enemy but without even a framework for understanding the world and their place in it. However imperfectly, the Cold War had for several decades offered a semblance of order and coherence. The collapse of Communism shattered that framework. Where there had been purposefulness and predictability, now there was neither.

Winning the Cold War brought Americans face-to-face with a predicament comparable to that confronting the lucky fellow who wins the Mega Millions lottery: hidden within an apparent windfall is the potential for monumental disaster. Putting that windfall to good use while avoiding the pitfalls inherent in suddenly acquired riches calls for prudence and self-awareness—not easily demonstrated when the big house, luxury car, and vacation condo you've always wanted are yours for the asking.

Similarly, the end of the Cold War might have given Americans pause, especially since the issues at hand were of considerably greater significance than homes, cars, and condos. At least in theory, the moment might have invited reflection on some first-order questions: What is the meaning of freedom? What does freedom allow? What obligations does it impose? Whom or what does it exclude?

Of course, Americans had been wrestling with such questions since well before 1776, their answers evolving over time. During the several decades of the Cold War, however, the exigencies of the East–West rivalry had offered a reason to throttle down impulses to explore freedom's furthermost boundaries. Except on the fringes of American politics, most citizens accepted the word from Washington that their way of life was under grave threat. In the pecking order of national priorities, addressing that threat—defending freedom rather than enlarging it—tended to take precedence over other considerations.

This is not to suggest that Cold War Americans were a compliant lot. They were not. From the 1950s, misleadingly enshrined as a decade of conformity, through the Reagan-dominated 1980s, domestic crises and controversies were constants. Among the issues energizing or enraging Americans were civil liberties, the nuclear arms race, mismanaged wars of dubious provenance, challenges to artistic tradition, left-wing and right-wing radicalism, crass materialism that coexisted with widespread poverty, and a host of simmering issues connected to race, sex, and gender. Yet through it all, a common outlook, centered on resistance to the Red threat, endured. For most citizens most of the time, the Cold War itself sufficed to explain "the point of being an American."

The collapse of the Soviet Empire between 1989 and 1991 robbed that outlook of its last vestiges of authority. Rarely, if ever, had the transition from one historical period to another occurred quite so abruptly, with such a precise set of demarcations, and with such profound implications. As if in an instant, the discipline that the Cold War had imposed vanished. The absurdity of defining reality as an either/or choice—Red or dead, slave or free, good vs.

evil—now became blazingly apparent. The impact on American ambitions and expectations was akin to removing the governor from an internal combustion engine. Suddenly the throttle opened up. The future appeared uniquely promising, offering Americans a seemingly endless array of choices, while confronting them with few evident constraints. Everything seemed possible.

Confident that an era of unprecedented U.S. economic, military, and cultural ascendancy now beckoned, members of an intoxicated elite threw caution to the winds. They devised—and promulgated—a new consensus consisting of four elements.

The first of these was *globalization* or, more precisely, globalized neoliberalism. Stripped to its essence, globalization was all about wealth creation: Unconstrained corporate capitalism operating on a planetary scale in a world open to the movement of goods, capital, ideas, and people would create wealth on a hitherto unimagined scale.

The second element was *global leadership*, a euphemism for hegemony or, more simply still, for empire. At its core, global leadership was all about order: Unchallengeable military might would enable the United States to manage and police a postcolonial yet implicitly imperial order favorable to American interests and values. Through the exercise of global leadership, the United States would enforce globalization. Order and abundance would go hand in hand.

The third element of the consensus was *freedom*, an ancient word now drastically revised. The new conception of freedom emphasized autonomy, with traditional moral prohibitions declared obsolete and the removal of constraints maximizing choice. Order and abundance together would underwrite freedom, relieving Americans of existential concerns about safety and survival to which those less privileged were still obliged to attend.

The final element of the consensus was *presidential supremacy*, with the occupant of the Oval Office accorded quasi-monarchical prerogatives and granted quasi-monarchical status. Implicit in presidential supremacy was a radical revision of the political order. While still treated as sacred writ, the Constitution no longer described the nation's actually existing system of governance. Effectively gone, for example, was the concept of a federal government consisting of three coequal branches. Ensuring the nation's prosperity, keeping Americans safe from harm, interpreting the meaning of freedom, the president became the center around which all else orbited, the subject of great hopes, and the target of equally great scorn should he fail to fulfill the expectations that he brought into office.

All these elements together constituted a sort of operating system. The purpose of this operating system, unseen but widely taken for granted, was to cement the primacy of the United States in perpetuity, while enshrining the American way of life as the ultimate destiny of humankind. According to the calendar, the end of the twentieth century, frequently referred to as the American Century, was then drawing near. Yet with the Cold War concluding on such favorable terms, the stage appeared set for a prolonged American Epoch.

This, however, was not to be. The United States wasted little time in squandering the advantages it had gained by winning the Cold War. Events at home and abroad put this post–Cold War consensus to the test, unmasking its contradictions and exposing its premises as delusional. Although globalization did enable some to acquire great wealth, it left behind many more, while fostering egregious inequality. The assertion of global leadership provided American soldiers with plentiful opportunities to explore exotic and unfamiliar lands, but few would mistake the results for even an approximation of dominion, much less peace and harmony. Instead, Americans came to accept war as habitual. And while the drive for individual empowerment removed constraints, it did little to promote the common good. An enlarged conception of freedom brought with it a whiff of nihilism. As for exalting the chief executive as a visionary leader, it yielded a succession of disappointments, before imploding in November 2016.

The post–Cold War moment, dating from the early 1990s and spanning the administrations of Bill Clinton, George W. Bush, and Barack Obama, turned out to be remarkably brief. By 2016, large numbers of ordinary Americans had concluded, not without reason, that the post–Cold War consensus was irretrievably defective. Globalized neoliberalism, militarized hegemony, individual empowerment, and presidents elevated to the status of royalty might be working for some, but not for them. They also discerned, again not without cause, that establishment elites subscribing to that consensus, including the leaders of both political parties, were deaf to their complaints and oblivious to their plight.

By turning their country over to Donald Trump, those Americans signaled their repudiation of that very consensus. That Trump himself did not offer anything remotely like a reasoned alternative made his elevation to the presidency all the more remarkable. He was a protest candidate elected by a protest vote. In that regard, the 2016 presidential election marked a historical turning point comparable in significance to the fall of the Berlin Wall a quarter century earlier.

The Age of Illusions seeks to understand what occurred between those two milestones. The quotation from the writer James Baldwin that introduces this book aptly expresses its overarching theme: promises made, but not kept; expectations raised, but unfulfilled; outraged citizens left with no place to stand.

1

AL, FRED, AND HOMER'S
AMERICA—AND MINE

Donald Trump was born in June 1946, the son of a wealthy New York real estate developer. I was born thirteen months later in Normal, Illinois. My parents, both World War II veterans, were anything but wealthy. At the time of my birth, my father was attending college on the GI Bill, with my mother, a former army nurse, working to keep our family afloat. In most respects, Trump and I had (and have) almost nothing in common.

Yet however the particulars may have differed, he and I were, in another sense, born in the same place, governed by certain identifiable propositions. Just then beginning to assume concrete form, those propositions informed post–World War II America. They described a way of life and defined what it meant to be an American. They conferred prerogatives and apportioned benefits. And not least of all, they situated the United States in the stream of history. Metaphysically, even though we have never met, Trump and I are kin—white heterosexual males who came of age at a time when white heterosexual males were granted first claim on all the privileges heralded by an American Century just then hitting its stride.

At the time of his birth and mine, ordinary Americans, whatever their race, gender, or sexual orientation, wanted nothing more than to move past the trials of the recent past, and the sooner the better. Mobilizing the nation for total war, a process directed from Washington, had taken years to accomplish. Demobilization, driven from the bottom up, occurred virtually overnight as the armed forces of the United States all but disintegrated. In the wake of Japan's surrender in September 1945, an eruption of civil disobedience unlike any in U.S. history swept through the ranks of the armed forces, an event all the more remarkable in that it was without structure or leaders. America's citizen soldiers were done with war and done with taking orders. With millions of GIs demanding to shed their uniforms and their loved ones echoing those demands, authorities in Washington had no option but to comply.[1]

Ever so briefly, the meaning of postwar freedom centered on getting out of the service and returning home. For vets, home meant the possibility of normalcy restored. While readjusting to civilian life might pose challenges, these could be overcome. The movie that dominated the Oscars in the year of Trump's birth offered assurances on that score.

Directed by William Wyler and written by Robert Sherwood, *The Best Years of Our Lives* tells the story of three veterans—Al, Fred, and Homer—back from overseas just as the sweet taste of victory is beginning to give way to the vexations of everyday life. All three are eager to return to life in "Boone City" while simultaneously wary of what awaits them there. All three are white, their ethnic identity or religious affiliation indeterminate. All three bear the scars of war, whether physical or psychological. Yet they exude a decency that asks for little apart from a fair shake. They are three ordinary men who have surmounted extraordinary challenges: one a small-time banker returning from combat as an infantry platoon sergeant in the Pacific; the second, a soda jerk elevated to the rank of captain who served as a B-17 bombardier flying missions over Nazi Germany; the third, a young enlisted sailor who lost both hands due to a shipboard fire.

In the course of the film, each of the three protagonists encounters severe trials, which he surmounts through grit and determination (along with the help of a good woman). Implicit in the film's gratifying message is this subtext: The hopes and dreams of these modest men are themselves modest. In the Middle America represented by Boone City, freedom isn't gaudy. It does not put on airs or bridle against received norms. Freedom imparts direction and confers purpose.

In an immediate sense, Al, Fred, and Homer expect no more than what they believe they have earned. As Fred, the soda-jerk-turned-airman, puts it, "All I want is a good job, a mild future, a little house big enough for me and my wife—give me that and I'll be rehabilitated all right."[2] But Wyler looks beyond whether or not returning vets can land a good job and afford a little house that's big enough. His story's several threads focus on this shared concern: whether intimate relationships shelved or torn asunder by war can be restored or, if not restored, replaced. Ultimately, he answers that question in the affirmative. By the time the film reaches its final scene, life's "best years" may still lie ahead, an outcome that validates the political, cultural, and moral framework to which the movie itself testifies.

The point here is neither to denigrate nor to idealize that framework, merely to acknowledge its appeal. *The Best Years of Our Lives* depicts postwar American freedom at its point of origin, when verities still retained a semblance of permanence. That upon returning from a war that has turned their world upside down Al, Fred, and Homer should want things put back in place, returned to what they had been when they went away, is hardly surprising. Neither is their yearning for stability, predictability, and normalcy.

In Wyler's Boone City, preexisting norms, not least of all those determining individual status, merit respect. "Freedom from" takes precedence over "freedom to." Almost of necessity, access to this unpretentious Eden is therefore limited, with women allowed only auxiliary membership and people of color all but excluded. Despite such restrictions—or perhaps because of them—this cinematic portrait of postwar America in its very first days resonated with those willing to spend two bits for a ticket.

And why not? The film was a mirror, a depiction of place and people that conformed to what large numbers of ordinary Americans wished to see as they left behind one period of history and embarked upon another. It offered assurances that, despite the recent upheavals, nothing essential had changed. The satisfactions of life centered on a stable marriage, an intact family, and honest work remained readily available, especially to those with the good fortune to have been born white, male, and heterosexual. As the critic Robert Warshaw, writing at the time in *Partisan Review*, put it, *The Best Years of Our Lives* offered a message of reassurance, "impressing the spectator with the dignity and meaningfulness of 'typical' American experience (his own experience) and making him feel a certain confidence that the problems of American life (his own problems) can be solved by the operation of 'simple' and 'American' virtues."[3]

From our present-day vantage point, we may doubt that the America depicted in *The Best Years of Our Lives* ever actually existed. Yet those flocking to see the movie when it was first released believed otherwise. Through the ensuing decades of the postwar era, the real-life equivalents of Al, Fred, and Homer, including my own parents, if not perhaps Donald Trump's, persisted in that belief. World War II—the Good War, even before that phrase came into common usage—remained a fixed point of reference, a lodestar. To preserve what the nation had won constituted a categorical imperative.

Foster and Henry Weigh In

Yet preservation was likely to require effort. Members of the policy elite were already insisting that the United States could ill afford to rest on its laurels. Just ahead lay new dangers that Americans dared not ignore. In the very week of Donald Trump's birth, for example, *Life* magazine, then at the height of its influence, featured a lengthy essay by John Foster Dulles, offering his "Thoughts on Soviet Foreign Policy and What to Do About It."[4] Here was a sign that Boone City's modest aspirations would not suffice.

Already exuding the authority of the secretary of state he was to become, Foster, as he was known to friends and colleagues, was a paragon of the Eastern foreign policy establishment. Less than a year before, World War II's triumphal conclusion had brought to fruition that establishment's fondest dreams, thrusting the United States into a position of global preeminence. Even so, Dulles's perspective was unrelentingly grim. Although Nazi Germany was gone and Imperial Japan vanquished, the United States faced another comparable threat. The Kremlin, he charged, was already pressing to create a vast "Pax Sovietica." Russia and America were on a collision course, with Soviet ambitions directly threatening all that Americans stood for and cherished. It was therefore incumbent upon the United States "to resist all expansive manifestations of Soviet policy." Failure to do so invited the ultimate disaster. "Assume that Soviet leaders cannot be brought to change their program," Dulles wrote. The inevitable result would be a "drift into surrender or war."

"If the past is any guide," he added, "it will be war." Averting such a terrible prospect was going to require concerted action or, as Dulles put it, "an affirmative demonstration that our society of freedom still has the qualities needed for survival." Here, a mere nine months after V-J Day, was a blunt articulation of the theme employed with notable success over the next several decades to keep the rabble in line: Dark forces abroad posed an imminent threat to freedom's very survival.

Dulles called upon Americans to confront this new peril head-on, making it "clear beyond peradventure that they are prepared to accept personal sacrifice to help keep freedom alive in the world." The real-life counterparts of Al, Fred, and Homer might think that their work was done. John Foster Dulles held to another view: The struggle for freedom was only just beginning. Sustaining that struggle required the United States to take the lead in opposing Soviet totalitarianism.

A devout if dour Presbyterian, Dulles framed the task at hand in spiritual terms. To overcome godless adversaries would require that Americans remain a God-fearing people. Unless disciplined by faith, he warned, freedom becomes little more than an excuse for "self-gratification," a temptation to which he suggested his country-men were notably susceptible. "Under such circumstances," Dulles cautioned, "freedom is dangerous." Only by tempering the exercise of freedom could Americans ensure its preservation.

Yet the magazine in which Dulles's sermon appeared preached quite a different gospel. *Life* was all about self-gratification. Dulles might urge his fellow citizens to submit to God's will (and, by extension, Washington's authority). For their part, the editors who assembled *Life* each week under the direction of publisher Henry Luce encouraged readers to do something else: grab with both hands all the happiness within reach now that the nation had survived both prolonged economic distress and global war. The issue dated June 10, 1946, containing Dulles's prescription for foreign policy, was no exception.

On the cover, the young actress Donna Reed posed at her most fetching. Inside was *Life*'s usual mix of stories, running the gamut from natural disasters (flash floods along the Susquehanna) and lurid crime (a murderer on the loose in Texarkana) to oddities (a photographic essay of university students engaged in an experiment "to test their kisses for germs") and vivid updates on the latest in fashion, fun, and politics.

The big spread of that week celebrated the postwar boom already transforming California into "the land of golden sunshine and golden opportunity." Vets were flocking to the state through which so many had passed during the war years. Bustle and promise were everywhere, *Life* reported. "Walnut groves and peach orchards are being grubbed out to make way for housing projects, movie theaters, [and] drive-ins." Fortune favored those with the moxie to seize it, including contractors converting abandoned streetcars into makeshift apartments rented out for $25 per week. The future of the golden state glittered—or at least it did for the white ex-servicemen whose entrepreneurial élan *Life* chose to highlight.

All of this was standard *Life* boosterism, as was the advertising copy that enlivened almost every page and reinforced the message of material plenty available to all. Bracketing Dulles's call to arms were ads for facial soap, shampoo, hair oil, mouthwash, cosmetics, deodorant, cologne, and other personal products. For those nursing complaints, there were remedies for headache, constipation, sunburn, and athlete's foot.

Other ads touted the latest in nylon stockings, women's undergarments, swimwear, and men's shirts that were "handkerchief-soft" while "richly masculine." For would-be sophisticates, *Life* offered whiskey favored by the "Men who Plan beyond Tomorrow." For the harried, there were cigarettes, one ad depicting an agitated mother confronting her misbehaving teenager. "When junior's fighting rates a scold," the copy read, "Why be irritated? Light an Old Gold."

Woven throughout was the promise of science providing Americans with longer, better, and more fulfilling lives. Thanks to

"Eugenics in a Cornfield," the Jolly Green Giant now guaranteed uniformity in each can of corn. With every kernel "bred right [and] grown right," it was, according to the copywriters, "Planned Parenthood" applied to agriculture.

Offering further fulfillment of that promise were the latest in household gadgets, which touted ease, convenience, and an end to drudgery. Kitchen appliances meant a "new kind of freedom." For diversion, *Life* promoted an array of radios, phonographs, and that novelty called television. For now, however, the automobile remained king—hence, the junked streetcars available for repurposing. A full-page ad in brilliant color proclaimed Packard's Clipper sedan "America's No. 1 Glamour Car!"

Elsewhere in the world, wartime exigencies had imposed rationing destined to continue for years. *Life* assured its readers that in America rationing was gone for good. John Foster Dulles might summon his fellow citizens to gird themselves for sacrifice, while choosing God above Mammon. At least implicitly, *Life* countered that sacrifice was becoming un-American. As for forgoing the delights of this world in order to gain entry into the next, that choice could be postponed or even finessed altogether.

William Wyler, John Foster Dulles, and the pages of Henry Luce's *Life* represented three very different and arguably irreconcilable notions of what postwar American freedom entailed or allowed. The Boone City version, a Norman Rockwell painting on celluloid, centered on safeguarding hard-won gains. Its rendering of freedom was tied to an idealized past. Dulles conceived of freedom in terms of impending ideological struggle. Preserving it—an iffy proposition at best—was going to require fresh exertions on a sustained basis. For the editors and advertisers of *Life*, in contrast, freedom was material, finding expression in the cornucopia of goods flooding the American marketplace now that the war had ended. Freedom centered on satisfying a continually evolving array of appetites and desires.

From our present-day vantage point, we may find fault with all three of these conceptions. None gave more than scant attention to what subsequently emerged as the two most troubling moral issues of the era, namely, the Holocaust and Hiroshima. Americans had experienced World War II as a Manichean event pitting all that was good against all that was evil. Now that Hitler had been removed from the scene and with the United States, however briefly, enjoying a nuclear monopoly, they were disinclined to entertain second thoughts about the war's origins, conduct, or legacy. What mattered most was its outcome.

These postwar versions of freedom fell short in other respects as well. In each, race, gender, and sexuality figured as the barest afterthought or not at all. None of them gave serious attention to environmental concerns or human rights, as we understand such matters today. As for diversity, inclusiveness, or multiculturalism—issues now at the forefront of American politics—even the terms were then alien.

The Intellectuals Say Nay

Yet whatever its shortcomings and internal contradictions, this three-faceted conception of freedom—preserving (or paying lip service to) received values, while resisting Communism and simultaneously embarking upon an orgy of consumption—defined the nation into which Donald Trump and I were born and in which we came of age. During the period stretching from the mid-1940s through the 1980s, as he and I passed from infancy and childhood into adolescence and then manhood, most Americans most of the time nurtured the conviction that the three versions of postwar freedom to which they subscribed could coexist in rough equipoise. That their nation should be simultaneously virtuous *and* powerful *and* deliriously affluent seemed not only plausible, but essential.[5]

"America First," the battle cry of those who prior to December 7, 1941, had opposed U.S. intervention in World War II, had fallen out of favor, seemingly forever. Yet the proposition that the United States should rank first in all things was one that most citizens simply took for granted. In their eyes, privilege became entitlement.

Not everyone agreed, of course. From the 1950s through the 1980s, a parade of writers, artists, and social critics questioned whether such expectations were feasible, compatible, or even desirable. In challenging the postwar outlook, members of the intelligentsia churned out books and articles, edited magazines, made films, composed music, performed, exhibited, organized, argued, and generally created a stir. Yet whether Al, Fred, and Homer paid much attention to any of this tumult is another matter.

Granted, from time to time, some particularly penetrating insight, often reduced to a catchy tagline, might find its way into the national conversation. Revelations about the pervasive authority of a *power elite*, the use of *pseudo-events* to manufacture reality, or the insidious implications of a *culture of narcissism* might cause a fuss in Berkeley, Cambridge, and Manhattan, attract passing notice in Washington, D.C., and even echo in the lesser provinces of Chicagoland where I grew up.[6] Yet the practical impact of these ideas was slight. Arriving at a deeper understanding of the forces shaping American politics or society rarely produced real change.

Ask Americans who grew up during the Cold War to identify Mickey Mantle, Willie Mays, or Duke Snider and chances are high that you'll get a correct answer. Ask them to identify C. Wright Mills, Daniel Boorstin, or Christopher Lasch and you're likely to get a blank stare. It's not that those American prophets lacked honor, even if they trailed well behind slugging center fielders in that regard. What they lacked was clout. So from the 1950s through the 1980s, while Mills, Boorstin, and Lasch wrote their books, the power elite flourished, pseudo-events proliferated, and the narcissistic inclinations of American culture deepened.

By no means am I implying that the bargain forged during the brief transition between World War II and the Cold War, with freedom defined as a mélange of traditional values, fierce anti-Communism, and go-for-the-gusto materialism, nurtured a sense of satisfaction or serenity among ordinary citizens. Indeed, Mills, Boorstin, and Lasch were among the writers who astutely discerned and tapped into a pervasive sense of anxiety, most obviously expressed in (usually suppressed) fears of World War III. During the Cold War, peace, prosperity, and the existing moral order were all valued, but each seemed fragile.

Nor am I suggesting that the postwar bargain was impervious to change. On the contrary, when pressures demanded accommodation, it proved remarkably pliable. Yet on matters ranging from the nuclear arms race and civil rights to free speech and sexual norms, change occurred in ways that left its essential elements intact. Through it all, the convictions to which Al, Homer, and Fred subscribed retained a privileged position. America remained a place where most people professed to believe in old-fashioned virtues while assenting to Washington's global campaign against Communism and simultaneously indulging an insatiable appetite to acquire and consume.

Only a single event threatened to overturn this precarious arrangement or, at least for a time, appeared to do so. That was the Vietnam War. As the central episode in the crisis known as the Sixties, the war divided the nation, and especially the baby boom generation to which Donald Trump and I belong. Yet the nature of that division was not what it then seemed. Only with the passage of time has its actual nature become clear.

From 1965 to 1972, when U.S. troops were fighting in Vietnam, the divide appeared to be between those who supported the war and those who opposed it or, within the ranks of the boomers, between those who served in Vietnam (as I did) and those who refused to serve. In retrospect, however, that pro-war/antiwar construct turned out to possess only transitory significance. The real split—the lasting one—occurred between boomers who saw Vietnam as an event requiring them to take a forthright stand, whether for or against, and those who saw the war as no more than an annoyance, not worth attending to except as a potential impediment to the pursuit of their own ambitions.

Of course, Donald Trump chose to affiliate himself with that second camp. Whether his multiple deferments, first for "bone spurs" and then for schooling, constitute a form of draft dodging may now be impossible to say.[7] What can be said with certainty is that on the matter widely considered to be the defining issue of the day, Trump was a no-show. Many of his contemporaries fought. Many others protested. He remained firmly on the sidelines, implicitly betting that, in the long run, the war wouldn't matter and that once it ended the country would largely revert to what it had been beforehand.

Trump was hardly alone in making that bet—and it turned out to be a shrewd one.

Battered but intact, the postwar outlook did survive the Vietnam War. Those who had remained on the sidelines paid no penalty. As the war faded into memory, much of the energy stoked by the events of the Sixties dissipated or was redirected toward trivial pursuits. The nation moved on, only superficially changed by the turmoil it had endured.

Dick and Ron Put Things Right

Nothing better illustrates the process by which postwar normalcy was restored than the presidencies of Richard Nixon and Ronald Reagan. During the Cold War, only three presidents managed to win two terms. Nixon and Reagan were two of those three. Their electoral success was well deserved: Nixon and Reagan were, in fact, the nation's two most consequential chief executives of the late twentieth century, even if more recent events have greatly diminished their legacies.

Many Americans today revile Nixon; as many remember Reagan fondly. For our purposes, their personal reputations are irrelevant, as are their lapses while in office. In retrospect, the Watergate scandal that forced Nixon's resignation has proven to be hardly more significant than the Monica Lewinsky scandal that, a quarter century later, led to the impeachment of Bill Clinton. Much the same can be said of the daft Iran-Contra scandal, a secret and illegal White House attempt to provide arms to the ayatollahs, that for a time badly tarnished Reagan's reputation. Whatever their crimes, misdemeanors, and misjudgments, Nixon and Reagan succeeded in shoring up the postwar bargain precisely when Vietnam and the Sixties had laid bare its vulnerabilities.

Nixon, the cynically pragmatic strategist, did so by reframing (and thereby perpetuating) the Cold War and by implementing a domestic reform program that bolstered the "vital center" of American politics at the expense of both the far left and far right. His breakthrough trip to Mao Zedong's China, undertaken in 1972, turned an erstwhile Communist enemy into a potential ally and converted the Cold War from an increasingly preposterous ideological crusade into a geopolitical competition with some plausible grounding in reality. Gone was the fiction of "monolithic communism," its place taken by a more concrete expression of what the United States was up against: the Soviet Union and its ragtag allies. With the possible exception of the Monroe Doctrine, Nixon's China initiative (among other things thereby opening the United States to China) remains the most creative gambit in the history of American statecraft.

On the domestic front, Nixon displayed a penchant for activism that bears comparison to Franklin Roosevelt's New Deal. Among his administration's major initiatives were: ending military conscription in favor of a so-called all-volunteer force; creating the Environmental Protection Agency and the Occupational Safety and Health Administration; signing into law the Clean Air and Endangered Species Acts; launching the "war on cancer"; embracing "affirmative action" to promote equal employment opportunity; imposing wage and price controls in an effort to curb inflation; abandoning the gold standard; expanding social security; and increasing federal expenditures on Medicare, Medicaid, and food stamps.[8]

Although Nixon may have been a Republican, he routinely defied conservative orthodoxy, going so far at one point as to assert that "we are all Keynesians now."[9] Not every program Nixon initiated achieved its intended (or at least advertised) purpose. Yet as had been the case with FDR, Nixonian reformism precluded more radical alternatives and thereby served essentially conservative ends. By August 1974, when he left office in disgrace, he had succeeded in deflecting the most prominent threats to the postwar bargain. Above all, while the Cold War had changed substantially, it remained the lodestar of American politics.

Reagan built upon Nixon's accomplishment by restoring to that bargain a moral sheen lost between the assassinations of John F. Kennedy and Martin Luther King in the 1960s and the spectacle of Watergate during the decade that followed. A seemingly resolute ideologue when he took office, Reagan proved to be surprisingly flexible, especially in accepting as genuine signals from within what he called the "evil empire" indicating that Soviet leaders wished to call off the Cold War. Yet in important respects, Reagan's entire presidency was a pseudo-event, its achievements based on the masterful creation and manipulation of images. Coming on the heels of "Tricky Dick's" criminality, Gerald Ford's blandness, and Jimmy Carter's puritanical disposition, Reagan's sunny demeanor and honed-in-Hollywood ability to strike whatever pose the occasion might require enabled him to reinvigorate faith in the postwar bargain. This was his preeminent accomplishment.

As president, Reagan touted Boone City values, reaffirmed the struggle that John Foster Dulles had charged *Life*'s readers to undertake four decades earlier, and assured Americans that prosperity was their birthright. These were the themes to which the "Great Communicator" returned time and again during his eight years in office.

Quoting John Winthrop, he asserted that it was the nation's calling to serve as a "city upon a hill," casting its light on all of creation. Citing Tom Paine, he told his countrymen that they had the "power to begin the world all over again"—refashioning that world in their own image. Parroting Franklin Roosevelt, he insisted that the present generation of Americans had a "rendezvous with destiny" and were therefore called upon to act. And all this, he assured the public, was in accordance with God's will. "Can we doubt," Reagan said while accepting the nomination of his party in 1980, "that only a Divine Providence placed this land, this island of freedom, here as a refuge for all those people in the world who yearn to breathe freely?"[10]

For Reagan, the glories of the American past offered assurances of an even more glorious future. By emphasizing the martial dimension of that past, he restored to the American story a sacredness that events of the 1960s and 1970s had diminished.

The sacrifices made by American soldiers at "Belleau Wood, The Argonne, Omaha Beach, Salerno, and halfway around the world on Guadalcanal, Tarawa, Pork Chop Hill, the Chosin Reservoir, and in a hundred rice paddies and jungles of a place called Vietnam," testified to the nation's willingness to fulfill its calling.[11]

In his Farewell Address, he returned to these leitmotifs a final time. Quoting Winthrop yet again, he admitted that "I've spoken of the shining city all my political life." He now described it as "a tall, proud city built on rocks stronger than oceans, windswept, God-blessed, and teeming with people of all kinds living in harmony and peace; a city with free ports that hummed with commerce and creativity."

"And how stands the city on this winter night?" he asked in conclusion. "After 200 years, two centuries, she still stands strong and true on the granite ridge, and her glow has held steady no matter what storm. And she's still a beacon, still a magnet for all who must have freedom, for all the pilgrims from all the lost places who are hurtling through the darkness, toward home."[12]

The actual record of the American past contains missteps, ambiguities, and horrors that Reagan chose not to acknowledge. His preferred version of that past was at best an artful fiction.

Even I knew that. Yet if Reagan's rendering of history did not ring entirely true, it qualified as eminently serviceable. And that was good enough for me. I was then playing a bit part in the U.S. Army's efforts to shed various afflictions picked up in Vietnam. Reagan endorsed (and generously funded) the project to which I, along with the rest of the officer corps, was deeply devoted. He provided the wherewithal that returned the army to health and made clear his conviction that the effort was a worthy one. I voted for him twice. So did most other soldiers.

My contemporary Donald Trump, now wheeling and dealing in the world of high-end real estate, was less impressed. In his 1987 bestselling book *The Art of the Deal*, he referred dismissively to Reagan as "so smooth, so effective a performer," while suggesting that at least some Americans were "beginning to question whether there's anything beneath that smile." That same year, he paid for signed full-page ads in the *New York Times*, *Washington Post*, and *Boston Globe* addressed "To the American People." Trump's manifesto, which cost him nearly $100,000, avoided criticizing Reagan by name. Yet he implicitly taunted the president for allowing Americans to be played for suckers. "Make Japan, Saudi Arabia, and others pay for the protection we extend as allies," Trump demanded.

> Let's help our farmers, our sick, our homeless by taking from some of the greatest profit machines ever created—machines created and nurtured by us. "Tax" these wealthy nations not America. End our huge deficits, reduce our taxes, and let America's economy grow unencumbered by the cost of defending those who can easily afford to pay us for the defense of their freedom. Let's not let our great country be laughed at anymore.[13]

Here Trump offered a glimpse of the America First neo-populism destined one day to vault him into the White House, even if conditions were not yet ripe for a populist revival. After all, Reagan was assuring Americans that the United States once more commanded respect and was fulfilling its providentially assigned role. So Trump's stunt made no appreciable dent in either the reigning postwar consensus or Reagan's own standing. Now approaching their dotage, Al, Fred, and Homer, of course, much preferred the self-deprecating Californian to the self-promoting New Yorker. When the Gipper left office, his approval ratings were sky-high, while Trump was plunging into a succession of ill-considered business ventures that lost millions.[14]

When it came to choosing Reagan's successor, Americans not

surprisingly elected the man who had loyally served for eight years as his vice president. In November 1988, George H. W. Bush crushed Michael Dukakis, the Democratic nominee, winning 426 out of 538 electoral votes and carrying forty of fifty states. Bush was a seasoned Cold Warrior, who could be counted on to carry on Reagan's legacy. And like each of his predecessors since Harry Truman, he was a veteran. Indeed, Bush had served with distinction as a naval aviator in the Pacific, where he had been shot down and dramatically rescued. His election signified a vote for continuity and for staying the course.

"A new breeze is blowing," he declared upon taking office in January 1989, "and a nation refreshed by freedom stands ready to push on." The way ahead seemed clear.

> We know what works: Freedom works. We know what's right: Freedom is right. We know how to secure a more just and prosperous life for man on Earth: through free markets, free speech, free elections, and the exercise of free will unhampered by the state.

In that regard, the new breeze served to revalidate what Bush referred to as "the old ideas," which he characterized as "timeless." Among the specific values he chose to highlight were "duty, sacrifice, commitment, and a patriotism that finds its expression in taking part and pitching in."[15] As had Reagan back in 1981, Bush inserted into his Inaugural Address a prayer to the Almighty. And why not, since Americans remained, in their own estimation, God's Chosen People?

One imagines Al, Fred, and Homer leaning back in their recliners and taking in the new president's words with a deep sense of reassurance. Not only had their fellow veteran ascended to the Oval Office, but he was forthrightly affirming what they believed.

The postwar bargain was clearly still in good hands. President Bush would be a faithful and attentive steward to all that America had represented since World War II.

In fact, of course, Bush would be the last veteran of that war, or indeed of service in any American war, to become president. As for the postwar bargain, it was on its last legs. In its place would emerge a new consensus, expressing the spirit of the post–Cold War era now about to dawn.

2

THE END OF HISTORY!

Few Americans who experienced the Cold War regarded it with affection. Fewer still imagined that it would ever end. So once beyond its sobering initial phases, highlighted by dangerous confrontations centering on Berlin and the Korean peninsula, the Cold War was not so much waged as managed. Dramatic rhetorical flourishes notwithstanding, both sides came to recognize that they shared a mutual interest in avoiding Armageddon, a point definitively driven home in 1962 by the Cuban Missile Crisis.

The challenges inherent in achieving even that limited objective appeared likely to continue far into the future, as would the rivalry pitting the United States against the Soviet Union, the Free World against the Communist Bloc, the West against the East. Presidents might express ritualistic hopes of achieving world peace, but the immediate task was simply to prevent the superpower competition from getting out of hand. Bipolarity seemed destined to persist forever.

Although tensions between the United States and the USSR eased in the mid-1980s, few observers possessed the imagination to conceive of a world in which the Cold War might become a mere memory. For national security professionals, especially those charged with thinking unthinkable thoughts about World War III, the one thought that remained truly beyond the pale was the prospect of the Cold War actually ending.

As late as 1988, even with President Ronald Reagan and Soviet leader Mikhail Gorbachev acting like best buddies, Pentagon propagandists were still insisting that the Kremlin's "long-standing ambition to become the dominant world power" remained intact, as did its commitment to "a basically adversarial relationship" dictated by the "Marxist dialectic." Having "amassed enormous military power, far in excess of what might be required for defense," the Soviets were even then continuing to "expand their military power," in large part to "satisfy their imperialist urge." So asserted the Defense Department, which detected no signs of "a renunciation or even an alteration of the inherently offensive Soviet military strategy."[1]

A year later, the Soviet Empire imploded, followed in short order by the Soviet Union itself. From Washington's perspective, 1989 represented Year Zero. Once again, as when World War II ended in a seemingly decisive victory, a new day appeared to be dawning. Once more, all things seemed possible, especially if you were lucky enough to be an American. And this time, there was no totalitarian antagonist to muck things up.

Yet as the Soviet Empire came apart, the rickety domestic bargain forged in the days of Al, Fred, and Homer came undone. As long as resistance to an alien ideology had numbered among the nation's priorities, that bargain had retained at least grudging legitimacy. Once the Soviets vacated the stage, its obsolescence—even its absurdity—became blindingly apparent.

While it continued, most Americans explicitly or tacitly accepted the proposition that the Cold War had centered on preventing freedom from being extinguished. As of 1989, that objective had presumably been achieved, inviting Americans to look beyond freedom's mere preservation and to consider instead its future prospects, which suddenly appeared limitless.

Annus Mirabilis?

The post–Cold War era opened on a note of euphoric optimism. By no means incidentally, members of the baby boom generation were just then ascending to the heights of influence. Leading members of that generation did not doubt America's destiny to bring freedom closer to perfection, even as the nation accrued still more power and wealth. Nor did they doubt their own capacity, now that the United States was no longer encumbered by the Cold War, to accelerate the fulfillment of such expectations.

Decades earlier, the theologian Reinhold Niebuhr had chided Americans for nurturing "dreams of managing history," while fancying themselves "tutors of mankind in its pilgrimage to perfection."[2] The outcome of the Cold War had now seemingly invalidated such concerns. History itself had handed down its judgment: America was its chosen instrument.

Such a conclusion required a carefully curated, not to say sanitized, interpretation of America's own past. Even so, this self-affirming perception formed the basis for a distinctive outlook destined to shape American politics and culture during the next several decades. The promulgation of that outlook was a top-down project. The voices that mattered belonged to members of the coastal elite, graduates of the Ivy League rather than the Big Ten, people who wrote for or subscribed to the *New York Times* and the *Washington Post*, rather than the *Cleveland Plain Dealer* or the *Indianapolis Star*, executives employed on Wall Street, not storekeepers from Main Street.

In that regard, the architects of this new post–Cold War consensus did not differ appreciably from the elites who had dominated American life during the Cold War or, for that matter, since the founding of the Republic. They were mostly male, mostly white, and with rare exceptions beneficiaries of a privileged upbringing. If they differed from their predecessors, it was in their relative indifference to religious tradition. Whereas their postwar predecessors had subscribed to a generic Judeo-Christianity, theirs was a strikingly secular perspective. They were not actively hostile to faith as such, merely oblivious to it. In their ranks, religion was akin to stamp collecting or raising orchids—a little weird to the nonenthusiast, but tolerated as essentially harmless.

In the autumn of 1989, with dramatic events making it apparent to all but the most obtuse or obdurate that the Cold War was indeed winding down, Donald Trump was focused on more immediate concerns. Business deals—efforts to buy American Airlines and to create a professional football league that could challenge the NFL—had not panned out as expected.[3] In any event, Trump was not much interested in attending to which way the winds of history might be blowing. His priority was self-promotion in the here and now. Dubbed "the People's Billionaire" by the *New York Daily News*, Trump had perfected the art of keeping himself very much in the public eye in ways that made him an emblem of the era.[4]

Defined by cynicism, selfishness, and excess, the 1980s had been a "Decade of Greed." So many observers of the contemporary scene had readily concluded. Attempting to capture the essence of a decade or a generation in a single word or phrase is a journalistic tradition dating back to well over a century ago. It originated as a game that anyone with access to a podium or a typewriter could play— entertaining without being entirely serious. Were the 1890s "gay"? Perhaps, but not noticeably more so than the decade that followed.

Were young Americans in the 1920s any more "lost" than their counterparts during the Thirties? No one could say for certain. But once begun, the urge to label persisted. And during the 1980s, as if by acclamation, greed got the nod.

Inverting the title of William Wyler's Oscar-winning film of 1946, the journalist Barbara Ehrenreich surveyed the period and called it *The Worst Years of Our Lives.*[5] If Wyler's *Best Years* had seemed to capture the essence of the immediate postwar period, its 1980s counterpart was Oliver Stone's *Wall Street*, released in 1987. Stone's film centered on a cutthroat business executive, Gordon Gekko, who operated on the principle that "greed is good." In comparison with Trump's real-life brashness and extravagance, the celluloid Gekko looked like a piker. Like Gekko, however, Trump embodied values that seemed, at least for a moment, to express something essential about the United States.

In October 1989, *People* magazine took a stab at explaining Trump's standing in contemporary culture while hinting at its potential political implications. With his outsize appetites and ambitions, according to *People*, Trump offered Americans something they were hankering for: a nation "built upon the creed that each individual among us can do anything if he has enough daring and drive." Here was Trump, "bayoneting through bureaucracy, knifing through neighborhood watchdog committees and zoning codes, hurling marble and steel and glass into the heavens" and thereby "reassuring us that our national myth still might be true." Ordinary citizens of the sort who read *People* evidently found solace in knowing that "swaggering, staggeringly rich American capitalists" were not an extinct breed.[6] Citizens who disdained that magazine and the cult of celebrity-worship on which it fed saw in the swaggering, staggeringly rich Trump all that they despised about contemporary American life.

Even as *People* was taking Trump's measure, however, a new trope was knocking the old one off its pinnacle. The decade of greed was ending in a year of miracles.

With startling suddenness, on the night of November 9, 1989, the prevailing zeitgeist gave way to another completely different one. Much as the stock market collapse of October 29, 1929, rang down the curtain on one period of history and inaugurated another, so, too, did the opening of the Berlin Wall. After the Crash, Americans kept drinking bathtub gin and listening to hot jazz, but the "Roaring Twenties" were over. Similarly, ending the division between East and West Berlin did nothing to diminish the avarice exemplified by the likes of Donald Trump. Yet attitudes and behavior hitherto treated as endemic now seemed merely incidental.

In Berlin, something wondrous had occurred, something that the interpretive template currently in fashion had not anticipated and could not explain. Those who assigned themselves the prerogative of divining the true meaning of events hastened to devise a new interpretive template. So it was that in an instant, the casting off of shackles by ordinary citizens displaced the profligacy of the superrich as the quality that ostensibly defined the age. As the buzzword du jour, *greed* was out, *freedom* was in.

Without missing a beat, members of the national media adjusted to the new script. The three commercial networks that dominated television news coverage wasted no time in explaining to Americans what it all meant. In an instant, the trio of men who anchored their rival thirty-minute evening news broadcasts converged on Berlin. By November 10, NBC's Tom Brokaw, ABC's Peter Jennings, and CBS's Dan Rather—well-groomed and well-spoken embodiments of the reigning American social order—were all reporting from the scene. By their mere presence, Brokaw, Jennings, and Rather affirmed that developments in Berlin qualified as a truly big deal: When all three network anchors appeared in the same place covering the same story, you knew that something requiring your attention was afoot.

For journalists and politicians alike, the Wall itself had long served as a made-to-order prop. Cinder block, barbed wire, armed guards, and German shepherds straining at the leash all combined to constitute a perfect metaphor for the Cold War. For this very reason, from John F. Kennedy ("Ich bin ein Berliner.") to Ronald Reagan ("Mr. Gorbachev, tear down this wall!"), a succession of U.S. presidents intent on scoring propaganda points had made good use of the barrier's visual potency, denouncing it as an affront to freedom, democracy, and human decency (even as they tacitly accepted its existence).

Now festooned with dancing, singing, *Sekt*-swilling, sledgehammer-wielding young Germans, the Wall was undergoing a radical reconceptualization before a worldwide audience in real time. "Tonight in Berlin," Brokaw explained, the celebration visible just behind him, "it is freedom night." It was "like New Year's Eve, only better."[7] Once a great "obstacle to freedom," the Wall, pronounced Jennings, had become "irrelevant."[8] "How do you measure such an astonishing moment in history?" he wondered.[9] Back in New York, ABC's Sam Donaldson announced that the Wall itself had "all but vanished" and, as a result, "freedom's light is shining."[10] Connie Chung of CBS affirmed the Wall's sudden transformation from an ugly symbol of repression into "a monument to the abiding dream of people to be free."[11]

Print commentary duly echoed such sentiments. According to *New York Times* columnist Tom Wicker, the fall of the Berlin Wall signified a "glorious victory for the West and the burial of Communism."[12] Reporting from the scene, *Times* correspondent Serge Schmemann wrote that events there seemed "to sweep away much of the common wisdom and presumptions of the postwar world." Whatever might happen next, the one sure thing was that "something essential had changed [and] that things would not be the same again."[13] According to the *New Republic*, "excitement bordering on ecstasy" constituted the only allowable response to the breaching of the Berlin Wall. "There are few times in history when you can say confidently that evil is losing ground to good," *TNR*'s editors wrote. "In East Germany evil is now in embarrassed retreat, and it is a retreat whose import can scarcely be exaggerated."[14]

Implicit in the festive TV coverage and the unabashed enthusiasm of print journalists was the question that Brokaw alone posed outright: "Is this the beginning of a new age?" Yet the overall tone of reporting left little doubt about the answer: Yes, of course it was. Something immense, definitive, and irreversible had occurred, with implications extending far beyond Berlin itself.

Initially, however, official reaction from Washington was notably muted. President George H. W. Bush was not quite ready to declare that a new age had dawned. In remarks to the White House press corps on the afternoon of November 9, he allowed only that he was "very pleased" by the day's developments. Pressed to speculate on what those developments might signify, Bush refused to take the bait. There would be no predictions and certainly no gloating from him. "[W]e are not trying to give anybody a hard time," he told reporters. "We're saluting those who can move forward with democracy. We are encouraging the concept of a Europe whole and free." Bush was pleased that among East Germans the "aspirations for freedom seem to be a little further down the road now." To a reporter puzzled that he didn't seem especially thrilled by such a "great victory for our side in the big East-West battle," the president replied simply, "I am not an emotional kind of guy."[15]

Bush's wait-and-see attitude annoyed Washington-based pundits. For syndicated columnists Rowland Evans and Robert Novak, the president's "subdued reaction to the seminal world event of the last four decades" suggested a troubling lack of historical imagination. The "Marxist surrender" in Berlin, they believed, heralded nothing short of "the reordering of the world."[16] A critique published in the *Wall Street Journal* similarly took Bush to task for his evident passivity. "As dominoes are falling across Eastern Europe," the United States was "sitting on its hands, trying to slow down the pace of change."[17] The situation called for yet more and faster change, with an American president's hand on the wheel and foot on the accelerator.

Washington Post columnist Mary McGrory likewise chastised the president for his evident lack of excitement. "Why did the leader of the western world look as though he had lost his last friend the day they brought him the news of the fall of the Berlin Wall?" she wondered. Bush's "stricken expression and lame words about an event that had the rest of mankind quickly singing hosannas were an awful letdown at a high moment in history." She was mystified by the president's inability to utter "a simple, fervent, 'Let freedom ring.'"*[18]

McGrory's dig, like those of other critics, implied the existence of some essential agreement regarding exactly what freedom signified. In fact, no such agreement existed, at home or abroad. The casual journalistic references to generic freedom also implied that the East–West conflict now visibly coming to an end had centered on ideology, the Cold War as a contest pitting those favoring freedom against those who rejected it. This qualified, at best, as an oversimplification. Such an interpretation was also to prove unhelpful.

---

* A quarter century later, Bush's son, George W., displayed none of his father's reticence. In 2003, as forty-third president, the younger Bush presided over the invasion and occupation of Iraq. Transforming that country into a stable democracy posed unexpected challenges. Still, in June 2004, when an aide handed Bush a note that read simply, "Mr. President, Iraq is sovereign," he scrawled this wildly premature response: "Let freedom ring!"

From the outset, the Cold War had been both ideological and geopolitical. At one level, it was a contest pitting capitalism against Communism, both of which came in myriad forms. Viewed from this perspective, the Cold War centered on seemingly irreconcilable ideas and values. Ensuring freedom's survival—perhaps even cautiously promoting its advance—defined the aim.

At a different level, however, the Cold War served as merely the latest in a series of great power rivalries dating back centuries. Viewed from this perspective, it centered on the pursuit of dominion. Asserting control, direct or indirect, over territory, resources, and populations—or denying control to the other side—defined the aim.

As the Cold War had evolved from the late 1940s into the 1980s, the rhetoric of freedom remained central to American political discourse. Among members of the intelligentsia, fads came and went, but none displaced freedom as the defining issue of the age. As the designated "leader of the Free World," each U.S. president was in turn expected to talk the talk. From Truman through Reagan, with differing levels of eloquence, none failed to do so.

As a practical matter, however, geopolitical considerations gradually eclipsed ideological ones. In that regard, developments occurring in the shadow of the Vietnam War proved crucial. When the United States aligned itself with Red China, forged an alliance with thoroughly authoritarian Egypt, and in 1979 threw its support behind Islamist insurgents in Afghanistan, ideas and values figured at best as an afterthought. William F. Buckley, the conservative editor of the *National Review*, might decry the opening with China as a "staggering capitulation" and mourn the loss of "any remaining sense of moral mission in the world."[19] In each instance, however, what determined U.S. actions was the prospect of enhancing American power at Soviet expense, regardless of any moral compromises and ideological contortions involved. Employed as a rationale for policy, freedom possessed surprising elasticity. It could justify almost anything; it prohibited virtually nothing.

Yet when the Cold War finally ended, memories of those compromises and contortions quickly faded or, at the very least, lost their salience. The way it ended—euphoric young Germans dancing atop the Wall—imparted to the entire Cold War a retrospective moral clarity that it did not deserve.

Scholars can speculate endlessly about whether the Cold War was inevitable or might have been avoided. What we can say with certainty is this: As it unfolded across several decades, it produced ruinous consequences. It fostered folly and waste on a colossal scale, notably in an arms race of staggering magnitude. It bred hatred, hysteria, and intolerance, creating conditions rife with opportunities for demagogues. It warped political priorities, subordinating the well-being of people to the imperatives of state security. Whether directly or indirectly, it provided a pretext for murder and mayhem, even if the victims tended not to be citizens of the United States or the USSR.[20]

The Cold War tainted everything it touched. As an episode in world history, it was a tragedy of towering proportions. So its passing ought to have called for reflection, remorse, repentance, even restitution. Yet the prevailing mood allowed for none of these, at least as far as most Americans were concerned. Instead, out of an era punctuated throughout by anxiety and uncertainty came a sense that a dazzling future lay just ahead.

Big Thinkers

An exquisitely timed depiction of that future, limning its essential contours, had only recently appeared. Just three months prior to the opening of the Berlin Wall, an article published in the *National Interest*, a Washington-based quarterly of meager circulation, had created among policy intellectuals a remarkable stir. The author was Francis Fukuyama, hitherto a little-known policy analyst. The title of the piece that vaulted him to instantaneous fame: "The End of History?"

The cautious question mark reflected an editorial misjudgment. Given the essay's expansive claims and eventual impact, an exclamation point would have been far more appropriate.

As a milestone in American intellectual history, Fukuyama's essay belongs in the category of writings that capture something essential about the moment in which they appear, while simultaneously shaping expectations about what lies ahead. Other distinguished examples include Alfred Thayer Mahan's "The United States Looking Outward," Frederick Jackson Turner's "The Significance of the Frontier in American History," and the poet Rudyard Kipling's "The White Man's Burden." Predating Fukuyama's essay by a century, each in its own way made an impact that greatly outweighed whatever literary merit it possessed. Separately and together they promoted the use of American power on an increasingly expansive scale.

Although today all but forgotten by the general public, Mahan (1840–1914) was arguably the most influential officer ever to wear the uniform of the United States Navy. Sailors like John Paul Jones, David ("Damn the torpedoes, full speed ahead.") Farragut, and World War II's William "Bull" Halsey achieved fame for their wartime exploits. Mahan's influence derived not from anything he did, but from what he wrote. A bookish Annapolis graduate with little affection for the sea but a prodigious talent for marketing ideas, he made his mark as a historian, strategist, and advocate of a more assertive approach to statecraft.

In a breakthrough article that appeared in 1890, Mahan identified "a restlessness in the world at large which is deeply significant"— this at a time when his countrymen had become accustomed to letting others tend to the world's restlessness. Such a passive attitude no longer sufficed, he insisted. "Whether they will or no, Americans must now begin to look outward."[21] For Mahan, looking outward meant that the United States should set aside any reluctance to involve itself in world affairs and assert its rightful place among the established imperial powers, a change in orientation necessarily requiring, in his estimation, the building of a great navy. In Washington, as the end of the nineteenth century approached, Mahan's message resonated. Here was an inkling of a strategy suited for a political class that was itself increasingly restless.

The interests of Frederick Jackson Turner (1861–1932) were scholarly rather than strategic. Yet the historical insight that made his reputation complemented the advocacy of Captain Mahan.

In 1893, just as Mahan was emerging as a full-fledged celebrity, the young Professor Turner, then teaching at the University of Wisconsin, gave a lecture that vaulted him to comparable fame. In Turner's case, the occasion was a meeting of the American Historical Association, convening in Chicago and coinciding with the World's Columbian Exposition there. Commemorating the four hundredth anniversary of the discovery of the New World, the fair was a grand event made to order for unveiling grand historical interpretations. Turner rose to the occasion. His reflections on "The Significance of the Frontier in American History" were concise, elegant, comprehensive, and compelling. Here was the distilled essence of American history from the founding of the English colonies all the way to the present: The inexorable westward movement of the American people had definitively shaped their collective character, imparting those qualities that made Americans distinctive (and implicitly superior).

Yet the recently completed census of 1890 had declared the frontier "closed." Speculating on the implications of this development, Turner reached conclusions that reinforced Mahan's. "The people of the United States," he wrote, "have taken their tone from the incessant expansion which has not only been open but has even been forced upon them." Only a "rash prophet," he continued, would "assert that the expansive character of American life has now entirely ceased." Movement had shaped that character. Turner felt certain that "American energy will continually demand a wider field for its exercise."[22] Americans would inevitably seek new frontiers.

A jingoistic British literary figure who took it upon himself to counsel his American cousins, Rudyard Kipling (1865–1936) knew just where to find those frontiers: abroad.

Kipling's fame as a journalist, poet, novelist, and writer of short stories spanned the English-speaking world. In the United States, his standing as a political commentator stemmed from a belief, then common in elite circles, in an identifiable Anglo-Saxon race engaged in a common civilizational project. Americans ostensibly numbered among the members of that race, even if they had long deferred to Great Britain and its empire to do whatever heavy lifting this project required.

The U.S. acquisition of a maritime empire in 1898, following a brief war with Spain, seemingly fulfilled Mahan's urgings and Turner's expectations. From Kipling, the war elicited a summons for Americans to start doing their fair share. Destiny, he insisted in his notorious poem "The White Man's Burden," now required the United States to "have done with childish days." Rather than merely tending to their own affairs, it was incumbent upon Americans to share the blessings of civilization with backward and "sullen peoples" in distant lands.[23] Duty called.

What the views expressed by Mahan, Turner, and Kipling had in common was this: Each discerned that an era of history had run its course. A new day was dawning, bringing with it new imperatives to which Americans would necessarily conform, whether they wished to or not. If wise, they would do so willingly.

Soon enough Mahan's ruminations about sea power, Turner's reframing of American history, and Kipling's race-based ode to empire insinuated themselves into the nation's collective consciousness. Distinctive but mutually reinforcing, their ideas shaped political attitudes and helped justify actions—for example, building a battleship navy, invading Cuba in 1898, and soon thereafter annexing the Philippines—that prior generations would have dismissed as misguided or outlandish. Mahan, Turner, and Kipling wielded influence not because their ideas were true but because they were timely. They filled a need, even before that need was fully formed and recognized.

So it was with Francis Fukuyama as the annus mirabilis of 1989 unfolded. In his case, the need was to decipher the implications of the postwar epoch suddenly and unexpectedly reaching its conclusion. As had Mahan, Turner, and Kipling before him, Fukuyama delivered what the moment required.

"In watching the flow of events over the past decade or so," he began, "it is hard to avoid the feeling that something very fundamental has happened in world history." The Cold War was winding down and with it the competition that had defined the twentieth century pitting "economic and political liberalism" against Fascism and Communism. The upshot was "an unabashed victory" for the West, Fukuyama asserted, and for "the Western idea" of nations subscribing to the principles of secular democratic capitalism. Efforts to devise "viable systematic alternatives to Western liberalism" had decisively and irrevocably failed. "Mankind's ideological evolution" had therefore reached its "end point" with "the universalization of Western liberal democracy as the final form of human government."[24] In short, "our" side—the West—had won. Game over.

As to who or what constituted the West, Fukuyama offered no specifics. The term, he seemed to suggest, connoted a cultural and intellectual construct rather than a conglomeration of nations. Yet when it came to power, the West clearly meant the United States, even if regard for allied amour propre made it impolitic to say so outright. To make the point more bluntly, without the United States, there was no West. By extension, only if the United States continued to lead and promote the "Western idea" would the history that was to follow "the end of history" remain manageable.

Fukuyama's hypothesis had two particular attributes that explain why it captured such wide attention. The first was its sheer grandeur. Here was a big argument, embroidered with references to dead European philosophers, that tied together past, present, and future to explain just about everything, while reaching conclusions that Americans inhabiting elite circles found gratifying. The second attribute was this: Fukuyama certified what the United States had professed to stand for all along, thereby obviating any need to consider doing things differently. The principal institutions of American power—Congress and the executive branch, the national security apparatus, banks and multinational corporations, universities and the mass media—could simply maintain the routines that had worked so well in delivering history to its prescribed terminus.

To be sure, not everyone joined in the applause. It is traditional among the American intelligentsia to make a show of dissenting from the latest theory claiming to offer the last word on any subject. Back in 1947 the journal *Foreign Affairs*, for instance, published "The Sources of Soviet Conduct," an essay purporting to explain Soviet behavior while prescribing a strategy of "containment" as a necessary U.S. response.[25] The handiwork of a hitherto obscure foreign service officer named George Kennan, it elicited instant acclaim. Soon enough, Kennan became the most famous American diplomat since Benjamin Franklin charmed the ladies of Paris.

Yet the essay also provoked sharp criticism, notably from the influential commentator Walter Lippmann, who insisted that Kennan was dead wrong.[26] Yet, paradoxically, such critical attention only enhanced Kennan's intellectual standing, while imparting greater weight to his views. For several decades thereafter, "The Sources of Soviet Conduct" would serve as an all-purpose rationale for U.S. national security policies. Not unlike the Bible, it would remain an abiding source of authority even when no longer actually read.

Of course, the term "containment" comes nowhere close to describing the actual pattern of U.S. behavior during those decades. At best, the views that Kennan expressed in 1947 imparted a rough azimuth to policies conceived in Washington. In subsequent years, however, periodic references to containment enabled functionaries implementing those policies to persuade themselves that they were engaged in an undertaking that retained a semblance of doctrinal consistency. Meanwhile, Kennan himself, appalled by the nuclear arms race and U.S. interventionism in places like Vietnam, was to disavow his own handiwork.[27]

Something similar occurred with Fukuyama and "the end of history." Critics wasted little time in picking the argument apart. Christopher Hitchens, the left-leaning columnist for the *Nation*, derided it as "self-congratulation raised to the status of philosophy."[28] Irving Kristol, founding father of neoconservatism, wasn't buying it, either: "I don't believe a word of it," he wrote, foreseeing a "whole series of rebellions against secular-liberal-capitalist democracy."[29] *Time* magazine columnist Strobe Talbott judged the hoopla evoked by Fukuyama's essay as evidence of "giddiness bordering on nuttiness."[30] Others piled on, some observers even speculating that Fukuyama had used the pages of the *National Interest* to pull an elaborate prank.[31]

Yet as with containment, although the hoopla soon faded, the basic claim persisted, acquiring greater authority with the passage of time. It did so not because "the end of history" conveyed demonstrable truths but because the implications embedded in that phrase were so eminently serviceable. Truth took a backseat to expedience. Much as had Mahan, Turner, and Kipling a century before, Fukuyama articulated an all-purpose justification for the American project precisely as the prior justification was about to expire. Nowhere was this new one more welcome than in Washington, D.C.

Fukuyama's theory not only sported a Made in the USA label, but was also custom-designed for the American market. Sure, Denmark and Australia might subscribe to Western precepts. Yet when the Cold War ended, Danes and Aussies did not thereby conclude that liberalism's success conferred any particular prerogatives on governments in Copenhagen or Canberra. Americans, however, believing themselves the foremost champions of the Western idea, claimed a lion's share of the credit for its triumph. To those occupying (or aspiring to enter) the inner circle of power, it was self-evident that the United States should orchestrate whatever history was to follow "the end of history." Having won, "we" were now in charge. By expounding on such expectations, Fukuyama invested them with credibility. In this way, he left an indelible mark on the emerging post–Cold War era.

As had Kennan, Fukuyama himself would in time disown policies devised pursuant to his own prescriptions.[32] Yet while his second thoughts are not without interest, they never really mattered. His essential contribution came in 1989 when he articulated the basis for a secular theology destined to shape American attitudes and actions for decades to come. If the post–Cold War consensus had a godfather, it was Francis Fukuyama.

3

KICKING 41 TO THE CURB

As the Cold War was ending, Donald Trump had other things on his mind. In 1990, his business empire was in trouble and his marriage to his first wife was coming apart.[1] Yet the embattled real estate tycoon bounced back with remarkable alacrity. In times of unforeseen duress, the absence of principle enhances flexibility.

Marrying his mistress (another union that would not last), he dumped assets that had become liabilities, stuck investors and other chumps with the losses, and returned the Trump Organization to profitability.[2] He acquired a range of new properties in Manhattan and elsewhere, all the while remaining the subject of tabloid fascination. All in all, it made for an impressive comeback.

I had no interest either in Trump's misadventures or in his achievements. As a serving officer, I had other concerns. In the summer of 1990, I assumed command of a regiment stationed in the Fulda Gap, long deemed a likely Soviet axis of attack into West Germany. Like Checkpoint Charlie in Berlin or the DMZ separating North and South Korea, Fulda was situated along a "Frontier of Freedom." Soon after I took command, the two Germanys reunited. With that, the frontier vanished. Fulda lost its geopolitical significance, becoming just another whistle-stop on the rail line from Frankfurt to Berlin. With the "end of history," Fulda—and my regiment—had become redundant.

As if to emphasize that redundancy, when much of the Germany-based U.S. Army headed for the Persian Gulf after the Iraqi autocrat Saddam Hussein seized Kuwait in August 1990, we were left behind. It became our mortifying fate to experience the ensuing campaign to eject Saddam's army from Kuwait by watching it on CNN. Only as units that had fought headed home to claim their well-earned accolades did we receive orders to the desert. Our mission was straightforward: establish a presence along a new "frontier," the border between Kuwait and Iraq. This I proceeded to botch. During our deployment, a horrific motor pool fire caused significant casualties and equipment damage for which I was quite properly held responsible. I had already had more than an inkling that I had chosen the wrong vocation. If I needed confirmation, here it was, in spades.

The termination of my soldierly career was personally wrenching. Yet it also proved to be liberating. Institutions stifle critical thought. Leaving the army offered an open invitation to reevaluate my understanding of America's history and purpose. I began to see things in a different light.

Donald Trump was not given to second thoughts. Even in the midst of trials that others would have found acutely embarrassing, he remained unabashed, undaunted, and unashamed. He pressed on.

The Insurgents of 1992

At the dawn of the post–Cold War era, President George Herbert Walker Bush, elected in 1988, seemed almost certain to win a second term. Yet voters decided otherwise. In doing so, they rendered judgment on the forty-first president. Not unlike a troop unit defending the Fulda Gap from invasion by the Soviet Eighth Guards Army after the Cold War had vanished, he had become redundant.

Bush brought to a successful close an era he thoroughly understood. His reward was to be sent packing as Americans judged inadequate his capacity to explain and deal with what was coming next. In one of the central duties of any president—to interpret the moment and divine its implications for the United States and the world—he failed abysmally. So in Bush's stead, Americans chose a prodigiously gifted politician who channeled the emerging post–Cold War outlook and made it his own.

Bush's interests and priorities were "out there" in the wider world, not "back here" at home. He never pretended otherwise.[3] Over decades of service to his country, he had acquired a depth of knowledge about the way the world worked—or at least about the way it appeared to work from the 1940s through the 1980s. Indeed, Bush came to office remarkably well versed in the practice of statecraft, the last American president to possess such qualifications.

With regard to foreign policy, Bush accomplished more than any president since Franklin Roosevelt and did so in a remarkably brief period of time. In managing the end of the Cold War, particularly in ensuring that a reunited Germany would remain firmly embedded in the West, he performed masterfully. In declaring that Saddam's annexation of Kuwait "will not stand," he made a gutsy call and put to rest nagging suspicions that he was a wimp who, as Gary Trudeau's *Doonesbury* comic strip charged, had "put his manhood into a blind trust."[4] Whatever else critics might say of Poppy Bush, Americans knew that he did not lack courage or steadfastness.

The ensuing military campaign mounted to liberate Kuwait not only succeeded, but did so with far fewer American casualties than expected. For a time, Operation Desert Storm occupied a place on the roster of history's all-time greatest victories. If not quite mentioned in the same breath with Gettysburg or Iwo Jima, it ranked right up there with the Battle of Manila Bay, Commodore Dewey's storied demolition of Spain's Pacific Squadron in 1898.

Bush had deftly presided over that desert victory, which boosted his approval rating to a stratospheric 89 percent.[5] Were that not enough, in the best traditions of U.S. gunboat diplomacy, he also deposed the Panamanian strongman (and former CIA asset) Manuel Noriega in an armed intervention of admirable brevity. All this in a period of slightly more than two years.

Even as he was racking up these victories, the president professed to glimpse better things still—a "new world order"—just over the horizon. In this new order, he pledged, all nations would be "freer from the threat of terror, stronger in the pursuit of justice and more secure in the quest for peace." All would "prosper and live in harmony." The result would be a world in which "the rule of law supplants the rule of the jungle," in which "nations recognize the shared responsibility for freedom and justice," and in which "the strong respect the rights of the weak."[6]

Now, every president from Franklin Roosevelt to Ronald Reagan had voiced similar predictions. Yet World War II and then the Cold War had relieved Bush's predecessors of actually being expected to deliver. Freedom served chiefly as a rhetorical device employed to distinguish our side from that of our adversaries. Peace functioned as a promissory note that presidents displayed while prodding Americans to make greater exertions in the here and now.

"In the future days, which we seek to make secure," FDR told Americans in 1941, "we look forward to a world founded upon four essential human freedoms." When that day arrived, freedom of speech and of worship, freedom from want and fear would prevail "everywhere in the world."[7] In the meantime, however, Roosevelt charged the nation to gird itself for war, which meant higher taxes and the prospect of sacrifice. Just shy of four decades later, in accepting his party's nomination for the presidency, Reagan declared that "first and foremost" among his goals was "the establishment of lasting world peace."[8] Yet chief among Reagan's immediate priorities was a huge increase in military spending to purchase an arsenal of new weaponry. Beating swords into plowshares and spears into pruning hooks would have to wait.

Events on Bush's watch suggested that the time for redeeming that promissory note had finally arrived. Yet here Bush came up short, unable to describe in sufficiently concrete terms the steps leading to peace and freedom, justice and prosperity. Americans responded by opting not to renew his contract.

Bush's speech in accepting the Republican nomination for a second term exemplified his shortcomings. On the cusp of an ostensibly new era, the president gave a tired old homily, laced with lame jokes and platitudes. Its most notable passage was a quasi-apology for having broken his promise never to raise taxes. "There's an old saying," he told the assembled GOP delegates, "'Good judgment comes from experience, and experience comes from bad judgment.' Two years ago, I made a bad call." While Bush did allude vaguely to a "new crusade, to reap the rewards of our global victory," he gave little indication of knowing what that crusade might entail. "The world is in transition," he declared. Toward what? On that, Bush seemingly had few clues. If the world was new, why was the prescription so familiar?[9]

Bush's principal opponent was Bill Clinton, the charismatic young governor of Arkansas, hitherto not known as an incubator of presidents. Were it not for the fact that the Cold War had ended and the American economy was slumping, Clinton would have stood little chance of turning out an incumbent. Unlike Bush, however, he had readily at hand an answer to just about any policy question.

Even so, like Bush, Clinton was a centrist, presenting himself to the electorate not as left-leaning—a label that had doomed Democratic presidential candidates from George McGovern to Michael Dukakis—but as forward-looking.

In outlining his blueprint for economic recovery, for example, Clinton rejected both the trickle-down dogmas of the Republican Party and "the old Democratic theory that says we can just tax and spend our way out of any problem we face." While the remedies that Clinton proposed were not necessarily original, they were detailed and specific: increased investment in education and training, adult literacy programs, national service (albeit on a voluntary basis), tax reforms "to give low-income entrepreneurs the tools to start new businesses," and "quality, affordable health care for all Americans"—all this and a balanced federal budget, too.[10] He also promised that on his watch the United States would remain the world's preeminent military power.

As a candidate, the patrician Bush came across as vague and detached, whereas Clinton projected both personal empathy and wonkish expertise. Trailing badly as Election Day approached, Republicans orchestrated savage attacks on Clinton's character, citing his efforts to avoid military service in Vietnam and rumors of frequent extramarital dalliances. The effort failed to break Clinton's momentum. In November, voters terminated Bush's lease on the White House.

The torch of national leadership had seemingly passed to a new generation. Yet while superficially persuasive, such an interpretation misses the deeper meaning of the 1992 presidential election. The real story was not of a sax-playing baby boomer displacing a genteel member of the Greatest Generation, but of insurgents hostile to the establishment that both President Bush and candidate Clinton embodied crashing the political scene.

Credit three individuals with touching off this insurgency. None of the three was destined to see his name grace the entrance to a presidential library. Yet each of them both anticipated and intensified the discontents that ultimately undermined the several propositions that shaped U.S. policy during the abbreviated post–Cold War interval. If not exactly voices crying in the wilderness, each became a channel of popular discontent that intensified as the fall of the Berlin Wall became not a turning point but a distant memory. Each in different ways helped pave the way for the political revolution that culminated a quarter century later when the election of Donald Trump brought the post–Cold War era to a crashing halt.

The first of those insurgents was Patrick Buchanan, a Republican operative turned pundit who tried unsuccessfully to deny George Bush his party's nomination. The second was H. Ross Perot, a wildly idiosyncratic entrepreneur who had made billions in the emerging world of information technology. In running for president as an independent, he sought, in effect, to subvert the entire political establishment.

Buchanan and Perot were bomb-throwers. Their declared intention was to blow things up. The third insurgent took a quieter, more oblique approach. Her name was Hillary Rodham Clinton.

Throughout her husband's presidential campaign, Clinton cultivated the image of a loyal, if accomplished and politically savvy, helpmate. Critics within the Republican Party depicted her as a radical, waging a covert campaign to overturn the existing social order on matters related to gender, family, and sexuality. Their tone tended toward frenzied hysteria. Yet their perception of what Hillary Clinton signified was substantively correct.

Buchanan came nowhere close to denying Bush his nomination for a second term. Even so, he earned himself a speaking slot at the Republican convention that August. Not given to accepting defeat quietly, he used that opportunity not to unify his party but to declare the nation itself irreconcilably divided. "There is a religious war going on in this country," Buchanan thundered. "It is a cultural war, as critical to the kind of nation we shall be as was the Cold War itself, for this war is for the soul of America." On one side in this contest were Americans devoted to traditional family values. On the other, he charged, were those committed to "abortion on demand, a litmus test for the Supreme Court, homosexual rights, discrimination against religious schools, [and] women in combat units."[11]

By delivering this memorably inflammatory speech, Buchanan all but hijacked the convention, as he no doubt intended to do. Lost in the ensuing hubbub, however, was the fact that cultural angst had not formed the primary basis of his challenge to Bush (and to Republican orthodoxy). Buchanan had actually built his campaign around the theme of nationalism. A skilled provocateur, he had resurrected the battle cry of those who until Pearl Harbor had opposed U.S. entry into the European war against Nazi Germany. "Our resolve is to put America First," Buchanan assured his supporters, "and to keep America First."[12] Here, of course, was the loaded phrase that Donald Trump was to revive a quarter century later.

Candidate Buchanan also offered his own distinctive take on what the passing of the Cold War signified. The fall of the Berlin Wall had "not brought with it an end to history," he argued. Beyond America's shores, a new world order was indeed forming, but not along the lines that George H. W. Bush or Bill Clinton envisioned. "The dynamic force shaping that world is nationalism," Buchanan insisted. Rather than vainly trying to remodel that world in its own image, the United States needed "to prepare for the new struggles already underway." An urgent first step was to reexamine "all the institutions of the Cold War, from vast permanent U.S. armies on foreign soil, to old alliances against Communist enemies that no longer exist." Why, Buchanan asked, "should the United States be required to carry indefinitely the burden of defending rich and prosperous allies who take America's generosity for granted as they invade our markets?" It was time "for a new patriotism, where Americans begin to put the needs of Americans first, for a new nationalism where in every negotiation, be it arms control or trade, the American side seeks advantage and victory for the United States."[13]

Ross Perot's candidacy was no less important, without ever being entirely serious. Entering the race in March 1992, he withdrew in July, only to reenter it in October. A political novice who had never held or even sought public office, Perot presented himself as the ultimate outsider, a folksy man of the people and advocate of direct democracy. His largely self-financed campaign defied all the usual conventions. In that pre-Twitter age, he employed televised infomercials as a means of unmediated communication with the public. Yet on Election Day, he appeared on the ballot in all fifty states and won nearly 19 percent of the popular vote. More important, however, his abbreviated appearance on the national stage injected into American political discourse a strain of economic populism that proved to be both persistent and, in the eyes of critics, toxic.

The themes of Perot's quixotic campaign meshed with and reinforced Buchanan's. He disdained bureaucrats and lobbyists, denounced government waste, and railed against inequitable trade deals. "While the Cold War is ending, another war is upon us," read the text of one Perot infomercial. "In this new war, the enemy is not the red flag of Communism, but the red ink of our national debt [and] the red tape of our government bureaucracy. The casualties of this war are counted in lost jobs and lost dreams."[14]

Perot's self-assigned mission was to awaken his fellow citizens to the way that ill-conceived policies formulated by "out of touch" officials beholden to special interests were gutting the American economy. The rich were getting richer while the wages of ordinary people were stagnating. "That's not fair," he contended. Under President Bush and his predecessor, "we got into trickle down economics and it didn't trickle down." "Millions of jobs" were being shipped overseas, replaced, if at all, by minimum-wage work in the service sector. If the United States was to remain a great nation, Perot insisted, "we've got to go back to building and making things."[15]

Perot's participation alongside Bush and Clinton in three presidential debates in October 1992 offered him an opportunity to expound at length on his message. In the first, he promised to purge the temple of the moneylenders, ridding Washington of "all these fellows with thousand-dollar suits and alligator shoes running up and down the halls of Congress." With no use for "the lobbyists, the PAC guys, the foreign lobbyists, and what-have-you," Perot was his own man and would therefore serve the people faithfully.

In the second debate, he explained his opposition to a proposed North American Free Trade Agreement, intended to remove trade barriers with Mexico and Canada. Bush and Clinton both supported NAFTA. So, too, did most economists. But not Perot. "To those of you in the audience who are business people," he explained, it's "pretty simple. If you're paying $12, $13, $14 an hour for a factory worker, and you can move your factory south of the border," you will reduce costs in a big way. "Pay $1 an hour for your labor, have no health care, . . . no environmental controls, no pollution controls and no retirement. And you don't care about anything but making money." The inevitable result? Jobs "going south." Perot was adamant: "We've got to make things here."

In the final debate, he took a swipe at the media for going "bonkers" over his proposal to consult citizens directly by instituting electronic "town halls." ("I guess it's because you will lose your right to tell them what to think.") Yet he concentrated his fire on what he called "the center of the bull's-eye": the deindustrialization of the American economy. If NAFTA became law, "you're going to hear a giant sucking sound of jobs being pulled out of this country," he declared, "right at a time when we need the tax base to pay the debt and pay down the interest on the debt and get our house back in order."

While Perot's candidacy centered on economic concerns, he joined Buchanan in expressing his wariness about Washington's growing appetite for military interventions abroad. It was "inappropriate," he said, "just because there's a problem somewhere around the world, to take the sons and daughters of working people—and make no mistake about it, our all-volunteer armed force is not made up of the sons and daughters of the beautiful people"—and "rush" in based on the whims of a few policymakers meeting behind closed doors. "I think if we learned anything in Vietnam it's you first commit this nation before you commit the troops to the battlefield."[16]

Perot's populism was a first cousin to the nationalism of Patrick Buchanan. Both were intent on salvaging what remained of Al, Fred, and Homer's America, even if members of the political establishment, to include the establishment press, viewed each of them as a cross between a loony and a crank.

Hillary Clinton's insurgency was of an altogether different character. Her purpose, veiled at first, was to hasten the destruction of Al, Fred, and Homer's America, in which white heterosexual males enjoyed privileges denied to those who were not white, heterosexual, or male. As she campaigned for her husband in 1992, it would have been impolitic for her to acknowledge her purpose outright. So the image that she cultivated and her handlers emphasized was that of a smart and accomplished but unthreatening woman desirous of nothing more than helping her husband do good things for all Americans. The persona she presented to the public was that of Mrs. Clinton, not Ms. Rodham.

In 1860, Abraham Lincoln had insisted that his purpose was not to destroy slavery but merely to prevent its further spread. Southern planters were not persuaded. They discerned—correctly—that electing Lincoln would spell the end of their "way of life." Radicalism was inherent in his candidacy.

So, too, with Hillary Clinton's arrival on the national political stage in 1992. Her gender, when combined with her ability and her ambition, made her a dangerous figure who posed a direct threat to the "traditional values" that late twentieth-century Republicans purported to cherish. Eleanor Roosevelt, the most formidable First Lady in U.S. history, had functioned as her husband's eyes and ears (and perhaps conscience), but she had not wielded power. With Hillary Clinton in the White House, it promised to be different. "Two for the price of one" was the tagline, meant only half in jest. If her husband won, she expected to enter the White House, in effect, as copresident.[17]

The Buchanan and Perot insurgencies differed from Clinton's in one crucial respect: Their purpose was to roll back while hers was to overturn. Buchanan and Perot charged leaders of both political parties with misapprehending what the passing of the Cold War signified, thereby putting long-term American security and prosperity at risk. The immediate imperative, they believed, was to repair and preserve. Clinton's aims were of a different order. As long as it had persisted, the Cold War had impeded social and cultural change. The removal of that impediment now created opportunities to redefine freedom itself. She was intent on seizing those opportunities, a proposition certain to elicit fierce resistance from those devoted to upholding the cultural status quo.

At one level, the 1992 presidential campaign was a contest

between two rival centrists—George H. W. Bush and Bill Clinton. At a deeper level, it marked the opening round of what was to become a full-fledged assault on all that the political center had come to represent, a campaign foreshadowing the future trajectory of American politics and culminating with Donald Trump's election as president twenty-four years later. In 1992, in other words, even before the post–Cold War consensus was fully formed, resistance was already forming.

4

GLIMPSING THE EMERALD CITY

In *The Wonderful Wizard of Oz*, L. Frank Baum's famous fantasy, when Dorothy and her companions reach the yellow brick road, the path to their intended destination seems wide open and welcoming.

> The road was smooth and well-paved, now, and the country about was beautiful; so that the travelers rejoiced in leaving the forest far behind, and with it, the many dangers that they had met in its gloomy shades.[1]

That Dorothy's friends should soon have their wishes fulfilled—the scarecrow granted a brain, the tin woodman a heart, the cowardly lion courage, with Dorothy herself returned to her prairie utopia in rural Kansas—seemed all but certain. The Wizard in whom they placed absolute faith need only say the word.

As the 1980s gave way to the 1990s, similar expectations swept through the ranks of the American intelligentsia. The United States was exiting a very dark and dangerous forest. The way ahead glittered and gleamed. And the road leading to a global Emerald City appeared smooth, well paved, and clearly marked.

As Americans emerged from the dark forest of the Cold War, four ideas—or enthusiasms—provided the basis for a new consensus that displaced the one to which Al, Fred, Homer, and their contemporaries had subscribed and to which their children and grandchildren had at least paid lip service. None of the four ideas qualified as entirely novel, yet together they combined to form an alluring package.

This Emerald City consensus differed from its predecessor in several respects. Yet far and away the most telling of those differences was this: Whereas the Boone City bargain had retained at least a nominal respect for limits, the Emerald City consensus centered on their rejection. The signature of the former was modesty; the signature of the latter, hubris, which found expression in expectations of material abundance on an unheralded scale, permanent military supremacy, a vastly enlarged conception of personal freedom, and a belief in presidential wizardry, if not exhibited by the incumbent, then expected of his successor. Binding this consensus together and lending it some appearance of plausibility was technopoly—a worship of technology, the deification of technique, and the conviction that problems in any sphere of human existence will ultimately yield to a technological solution.[2]

Superpower, Super-Stories

"I am a big believer in the idea of the super-story, the notion that we all carry around with us a big lens, a big framework, through which we look at the world, order events, and decide what is important and what is not." So wrote *New York Times* columnist Thomas L. Friedman in the prologue to a 2002 compendium of his columns.[3]

Friedman had made a career, and a good one at that, out of flogging one super-story after another. That he enjoyed success in doing so stemmed in part from his talents as a troubadour of power, but also from the fact that the years following the end of the Cold War were particularly accommodating to big lens/big framework theories purporting to divine the future.

The passing of the Cold War brought with it the conviction that whatever was to come next was going to be not only different, but wondrous. This belief was especially strong among self-appointed interpreters of the American scene, notably politicians, journalists, and academics with connections to Washington.

In that regard, Francis Fukuyama served as an inadvertent John the Baptist, making straight the way for various messiahs purporting to illuminate the new order that the triumph of secularized liberal democratic capitalism was bringing into view. Friedman was prominent among those seeking to harmonize the several elements of this new order into a single marketable super-story, thereby dignifying the era to come with a simulacrum of intellectual coherence.

The name commonly applied to the first such element was globalization, an elusive term with a myriad definitions depending on purpose or perspective. To some, globalization suggested "the compression of the world" and the emergence of a collective consciousness.[4] According to this view, the passing of Cold War divisions and the proliferation of information technology pointed toward greater interdependence and enhanced human solidarity. Planet Earth was becoming a "global village."[5] Implicit in this formulation were expectations of those villagers sooner or later coalescing around Western notions of modernity, where Western meant American and modernity implied submission to the dictates of the marketplace.

The adoption of globalization to describe this process implied that something unprecedented was afoot—something crying out for linguistic razzle-dazzle. The promotion of globalization included a generous element of hucksterism—the equivalent of labeling a large cup of strong coffee a "grande dark roast," while referring to the server handing it to you as a "barista." The argot might convey a certain cachet, but it's still the same old beverage.

Here, Friedman emerged as the razzle-dazzler par excellence. As he put it in his immodestly titled "Manifesto for a Fast World," globalization signified "the spread of free-market capitalism to virtually every country in the world." It was all rather simple really: "The more you let market forces rule and the more you open your economy to free trade and competition, the more efficient and flourishing your economy will be." Globalization promised to transform humanity's relationship with the material world, satisfying and then enlarging appetites for consumption in a never-ending cycle, while marginalizing or extinguishing phenomena suspected of impeding that process.

Such expectations were not quite as original as their promoters professed to believe. More than a century earlier, for example, Harvard's William Graham Sumner, the most influential American social scientist of his day, had described the existing economy as one in which "we earn our living daily by contributing to satisfy the wants of thousands scattered all over the world," while "our wants are satisfied instantaneously and regularly by the cooperation of thousands of people all over the world whom we have never seen or heard of." According to Professor Sumner, anticipating Friedman, "The whole industry and commerce of the world" functioned as a "great system" that was in constant flux even as it simultaneously adhered to certain ironclad rules.[6]

In fact, the circulation of goods, capital, technology, ideas, and people around the world had been ongoing for centuries, although the depth, breadth, and impact of interaction varied according to circumstance. The Columbian Exchange initiated in 1492, involving, among other things, plants, animals, bacteria, and deadly diseases, offers one notable illustration.[7] Europe's subsequent incorporation of the "New World" into a system of rival empires during the sixteenth century offers another. So, too, does the subsequent amalgamation of thirteen English colonies into a restless republic intent on exporting a white Anglo-Saxon Protestant brand of civilization even as it absorbed (and domesticated) a wide array of foreign influences. In other words, even before the United States had emerged as a great power, Americans were deeply enmeshed in activities that today fall under the rubric of globalization.

Some had benefited from the process, acquiring wealth and power. Others had suffered from it, the results ranging from cultural disintegration to virtual extermination. Globalization had redistributed power, but it had hardly produced brotherly love. Certainly it had not prevented the titanic conflicts that made the twentieth century a charnel house.

A balanced or measured view of prior iterations of globalization might have induced caution in anyone contemplating what the wholehearted embrace of such a Darwinian process was likely to produce now that the era of bipolarity had ended. Yet the post–Cold War temperament was not conducive to caution. The fall of the Berlin Wall had ostensibly wiped the slate clean. After all, a world divided in two had suddenly become one. The question now presenting itself was how to turn to good advantage the breathtaking opportunities created by the passing of the Cold War.

In policy circles, it seemed self-evident that unfettered globalization held the key to creating a new and better world order, much as following World War II it had seemed self-evident that the U.S. atomic monopoly held the key to preventing World War III. Not everyone had then agreed and skeptics were allowed their say. Yet dissent, even coming from the scientists who had created the bomb and soon thereafter were calling for its abolition, had a negligible effect on policy. In effect, opposition was pro forma. In similar manner, with naysayers heard and ignored, globalization became the cornerstone of Washington's post–Cold War super-story.

Crucially, in its latest reincarnation, globalization was—or appeared to be—an inherently American project. "Globalization is U.S.," as Friedman put it with characteristic insouciance. "We Americans are the apostles of the Fast World, the prophets of the free market and the high priests of high tech." Globalization was like baseball or basketball: It was an American game; we had invented it; we were now offering it to others and might even allow them to play, assuming they adhered to our rules. Yet absent extreme laziness or outright stupidity, the competition was ours to win.[8]

During the Cold War, the West had provided a venue for experimenting with the concept of globalization on a limited scale. In effect, the so-called Free World served as a prototype for the way a globalized world might work, with barriers to trade, travel, and investment reduced and norms governing interaction between states and citizens codified.

By fostering a shared (if uneven) prosperity, these arrangements had enabled the United States and its allies to best the Soviets and their allies. Replicating on a planetary scale the success achieved during the Cold War seemed an obvious next step. What had worked in the West would surely work in the East and the South as well. Although in the near term the embrace of globalization might create winners and losers, losers would have both incentive and opportunity to retool and get with the program.

Truth to tell, no real alternative existed. So, at least, august figures insisted. As Alan Greenspan put it in 2007, "The world is governed by market forces." The former Federal Reserve chairman offered that blunt judgment without caveats or exceptions. It was, therefore, incumbent upon senior officials, whether elected or appointed, to recognize and defer to this immutable reality. Indeed, Greenspan deemed it "fortunate" that "policy decisions in the U.S. have been largely replaced by global market forces," so much so that "national security aside, it hardly makes any difference" whom Americans installed in the White House.[9]

Yet the creation of such an open world, accelerating and intensifying the movement of goods, capital, technology, ideas, and people, meant more than simply greater material abundance. Ultimately, an open world giving free rein to American-style capitalism would lay the basis for—would even require—a Pax Americana, in which American values would flourish and Americans would enjoy pride of place.

Some contrarians suggested otherwise, predicting that globalization was likely to breed conflict rather than solidarity. In a world of "fast music, fast computers, and fast food," the sociologist Benjamin Barber wrote in 1992, demands for "integration and uniformity" might well elicit a violent backlash, leading to the "retribalization of large swaths of humankind." Rather than villagers living in harmony, rival tribes waging "jihad in the name of a hundred narrowly conceived faiths against every kind of interdependence" was a more likely prospect.[10]

Yet the conception of globalization that found particular favor among American policy intellectuals and policymakers was a positive one, emphasizing its potential to promote economic growth in the aggregate. Only a minority, H. Ross Perot offering one example, suggested that globalization might ultimately work to the disadvantage of ordinary Americans. Just about no one foresaw the possibility of those injured and left behind rising up to reject its premises.

Preferring Swords to Plowshares

The second element of the Emerald City consensus related to statecraft and the means of policing this Pax. Its theme was global leadership.

Globalization requires order. Only where there is stability, predictability, and adherence to specified norms can openness flourish. By extension, globalization demands some mechanism to guarantee openness and enforce the rules. In the wake of the Cold War, American policy elites concluded with something close to unanimity that it was incumbent upon the United States to do just that, relying on U.S. military might to guarantee and enforce. That the capacity, prowess, and durability of the nation's armed services were sufficient unto the task was, like the faith invested in globalization, taken as a given.

From a military perspective, then, the Cold War never really ended; instead, it underwent a metamorphosis, giving rise to new expectations and imposing fresh requirements. After the fall of the Berlin Wall, U.S. forces did not stand down. "Mission accomplished" did not mean mission concluded. With the collapse of the Soviet Empire, the principal rationale for garrisoning the world—defending against the Red Threat—may have vanished. Even so, as Washington elites saw it, the United States had no choice but to maintain its global military presence.

Perpetuating the expansive military "footprint" that had evolved during the Cold War evoked minimal controversy. That the troops stationed in Europe, Asia, and other distant stations should now return home never received serious consideration. The disappearance of the Red Threat did trigger a flurry of domestic speculation about possibly reducing U.S. military spending by a notch or two, thereby allowing Americans to claim a "peace dividend." And in the early 1990s, the Pentagon budget did modestly decline.[11] Yet with other nations seizing the opportunity to shrink their own forces, in many cases drastically, the U.S. share of worldwide military expenditures actually increased.[12] Indeed, no other country even came close.

For those keen to preserve the existing national security apparatus, threat diminution did pose a problem of sorts. For decades, estimates of Soviet military outlays had provided the benchmark for calculating "how much is enough." The budgetary and bureaucratic implications of those estimates had created compelling motives to embellish or exaggerate. When the facts available did not suffice to support desired conclusions, scaremongers could be counted on to make up the deficit. The spurious "bomber gap" of the mid-1950s and the "missile gap" touted by presidential candidate John F. Kennedy later that same decade offered particularly infamous examples of that impulse. That Pentagon estimates of Soviet military capabilities tended to be long on "poetry" and short on "plumbing" was widely recognized, deplored by a few, tacitly accepted by most.[13]

With the passing of the Cold War, however, citing the putative danger posed by ten-foot-tall Ivans as a gauge for sizing military budgets no longer worked. Soon enough, the stewards of national security devised an alternative justification for American military power, one that emphasized capabilities to be employed, rather than threats to be contained.

The problem of averting Armageddon having seemingly been solved, the task now confronting the military was to foster a new and better global order. "Shaping the international environment" was the anodyne phrase devised to frame this undertaking. From a budgetary perspective, the value, indeed the genius, of the phrase lay in its elasticity. Applied to military affairs, traditional terms such as "deter," "defend," and "destroy" meant something concrete and specific. "Shaping," by comparison, was amorphous. Requiring nothing in particular, it could permit just about anything. It promised to enlarge American freedom of action. As far as the national security apparatus and all those dependent upon the largesse of the military-industrial complex were concerned, this was its chief attribute. Here was a gift that promised to keep on giving.

As it embarked upon the post–Cold War era, the United States faced few pressing dangers. Risks appeared manageable. In such circumstances, self-restraint seemed tantamount to timidity. So in national security circles, the collective mindset began tilting toward activism. With minimal ceremony, the principal raison d'être of the American military establishment was thereby inverted.

That circumstances now allowed the armed forces of the United States to do more meshed seamlessly with emerging convictions that they could and by extension should do more. Converting opportunity into imperative was the belief that the United States had achieved or could readily achieve unquestioned military supremacy. Here, too, something akin to the end of history was at hand.

In the historical narrative that most Americans carry in their heads, past wars help establish a basic chronology. "History is a bath of blood," philosopher William James observed at the outset of a century that seemed to demonstrate the truth of his dictum.[14] If only subconsciously, Americans have long tended to organize the past in Jamesean terms. Linked together, America's wars provide a narrative spine to what might otherwise appear to be simply "one damn thing after another." Starting with Lexington and Concord in the spring of 1775, they chart the nation's rise to greatness.

To be sure, those wars do not all enjoy equal standing. As enshrined in memory—perhaps as measured by the frequency with which they attract the attention of Hollywood—they vary in weight or significance. More than a few have been altogether forgotten.[15] A ranking of those deemed worth remembering would have the Civil War and World War II at the very top, occupying a category all their own, followed by the American Revolution, Korea, and Vietnam, with everything else, including wars with Mexico and Spain and U.S. participation in the European war of 1914–1918, consigned to footnote status.

Of course, the most recent episode in that sequence interrupted—
for a time appeared to refute—the narrative of ascent, which went a
long way toward explaining why Americans found Vietnam so difficult to digest. Unlike, say, the War of 1812, a debacle redeemed
by Andrew Jackson's belated victory at New Orleans, or the campaign to liberate Cuba in 1898, where the colorful heroics of Teddy
Roosevelt's Rough Riders partially diverted attention from gross
military ineptitude, spinning Vietnam as a success proved impossible.

Considered in this context, the end of the Cold War offered the
possibility of reclassifying Vietnam as a mere aberration. The fall
of the Berlin Wall restored the narrative of national ascent. Rather
than exposing something dark and terrible about America itself,
Vietnam became no more than an unfortunate setback in what
most Americans persisted in seeing as a good-news story.

Yet the role specifically attributed to military power in concluding the Cold War did more than simply allow Americans to get
over residual Vietnam-induced angst. According to an interpretation
that gained wide favor in Washington, superior military might had
played a decisive role in determining the final outcome. The United
States had "won" a metaphorical "war" of immense consequence
because the enemy had come to realize that further struggle was
futile. With U.S. military capabilities growing more awesome by the
day, Soviet leaders were left with a single option: Give up. In effect,
without firing a shot, the United States had vanquished its adversary.
Here was an achievement without precedent—an epic victory that
had not entailed a bath of blood. In all of military history, nothing
like this had ever happened before—so, at least, leading figures in
the national security apparatus persuaded themselves.

As if to corroborate this verdict, hard on the heels of the Cold
War came the Persian Gulf War of 1990–1991, a grand exclamation point tacked onto the end of a momentous decade. Even as

intellectuals were reflecting on what the "end of history" might signify, military history was resuming, albeit in ways that seemed to affirm Fukuyama's hypothesis. The conclusion of the Cold War showed that the U.S. military could win without fighting. The Persian Gulf War showed not only that America's armed forces could still fight, but that they were seemingly invincible.

So the nation's military narrative added a chapter: After Vietnam there now came Desert Storm. The latter did not expunge the former. Yet the military failure in Southeast Asia now lost much of its relevance. By putting a ragtag Iraqi army to flight, the United States had emphatically "kicked the Vietnam syndrome," as President George H. W. Bush put it at the time. With that, reticence about using force evaporated, especially in elite circles. In a post–Cold War world that awaited shaping, America's manifest superiority in all things military positioned it to do whatever needed to be done.

America's armed forces now stood alone in solitary splendor. Accepted with near unanimity, this "fact" presented the United States with a dazzling opportunity. If Americans chose to maintain their unambiguous military preeminence, others might come to see armed conflict as pointless. Nations would cease to engage in expensive arms races. History itself would cease to be a bath of blood. To many in Washington, especially those fancying themselves cut from the same cloth as Otto von Bismarck or Henry Kissinger, the logic was compelling—and nicely suited to advancing their own ambitions.

Much as the Corsican Napoleon Bonaparte crowned himself Emperor of the French in 1804, members of the American political elite after 1989 conferred on the United States the title of "sole superpower." That phrase and others like it—"indispensable nation" offers another example—implied the exercise of imperial prerogatives on a truly global scale. More than a few observers from abroad concurred. The foreign minister of the French Republic, considerably reduced since the heyday of Napoleon, even coined a new word to describe America's unprecedented status: *hyperpuissance* or hyperpower.

With America's singular standing among the world's nations came singular responsibilities. Writing in *Foreign Affairs* in 1992, General Colin Powell, chairman of the Joint Chiefs of Staff and then ranked alongside George Washington and George C. Marshall in the pantheon of American military greats, made the point directly:

> No other nation on earth has the power we possess. More important, no other nation on earth has the trusted power that we possess. We are obligated to lead. If the free world is to harvest the hope and fulfill the promise that our great victory in the Cold War has offered us, America must shoulder the responsibility of its power. The last best hope of earth has no other choice. We must lead.[16]

Harvesting the hope (or seizing the opportunity) created by the absence of any serious rival had a large military aspect. Under the terms of the Boone City consensus, the imperatives of defense and deterrence had provided a rationale for amassing formidable military capabilities. A receding Soviet threat now undercut that rationale. So authorities in Washington promptly redefined the purpose of the U.S. military establishment.

Although the great standoff with Communism may have ended, it turned out that America's armed might was needed more than ever. As Powell put it, "Our arms must be second to none." Indeed, "second to none" understated the requirement. For Powell and others in the national security establishment, only a position of uncontested military dominion would enable the United States to fulfill its self-assigned obligations.

Viewed from our present vantage point, with U.S. forces in recent decades having experienced many more disappointments than decisive victories, the very idea of pursuing military supremacy might seem a dicey, even megalomaniacal proposition. Yet at the time, defining leadership as a function of matchless military might was about as controversial as referring to Elvis as "the King." Having succumbed to an infatuation with all things military, members of the American political class were ripe for self-deception. So, too, were more than a few citizens whose comprehension of military affairs extended no farther than movies or video games.

As long as the United States Army, Navy, Air Force, and Marine Corps maintained their collective reputation for invincibility, these expectations appeared eminently plausible. After all, who was there to say nay? Who would dare challenge a Pax backed by the American military juggernaut?

Indeed, in the early 1990s, popular confidence in the effectiveness of America's armed forces had reached stratospheric heights, comparable perhaps to German confidence in the Wehrmacht in 1940 after the fall of France or Confederate belief in Lee's Army of Northern Virginia prior to Gettysburg. For Germans and Southerners, such inflated confidence underwrote recklessness and paved the way for ignominious defeat. A similar, if slow-motion chastening awaited twenty-first-century American militarists. At the time, however, General Powell was merely saying what the typical *Foreign Affairs* reader was eager to believe.

Not by chance or coincidence, there emerged from within national security circles a blueprint for sustaining U.S. military dominance, not simply in the short term but far into the future. This was the Revolution in Military Affairs or RMA.[17]

The RMA stands in relation to war as globalization stood in relation to political economy: It purported to describe the culmination of a long evolutionary march toward perfection. Globalization promised to reduce the uncertainties that had plagued the operation of the market. In similar manner, the RMA was expected to reduce—and perhaps even eliminate—uncertainties that had long plagued the conduct of war and had made it such a risky proposition. The nation that seized the opportunities it presented would enjoy decisive advantages over any and all adversaries.

By the 1990s, the theorists who dreamed up the RMA had convinced themselves that old-fashioned warfare, which relied on large numbers of soldiers and massive arsenals of destructive but not terribly accurate weapons, was going the way of the steam locomotive or the typewriter. A new model of high-tech warfare, waged by highly skilled professionals equipped with "smart" weapons, had begun to emerge, with the Pentagon far out in front of any potential competitor in appreciating the significance of this military revolution.

This image of transformed and transformational war derived from, even as it reinforced, the technology-hyped mood that characterized the post–Cold War era as a whole. By common consent, the defining characteristics of this new Information Age were speed, control, and choice. Even as it was empowering the individual, information technology was reducing the prevalence of chance, surprise, and random occurrences. Henceforth, everything relevant could be known and, if known, could be taken into account, lessening, if not eliminating, uncertainty, risk, waste, and error and producing quantum improvements in efficiency and effectiveness.

The potential for grafting information technology onto armed conflict—long viewed as an area of human endeavor especially fraught with uncertainty, risk, waste, and error—appeared particularly alluring. Given access to sufficient information, warrior-statesmen could arrest war's tendency to become uncontrollable. Swiftness, stealth, agility, and precision would characterize the operations of truly modern armies. Henceforth, economy, predictability, and political relevance would constitute the hallmarks of war. Enhancing the appeal of this vision for members of the American officer corps was the implicit expectation that embracing the RMA would preclude the possibility of another Vietnam. The RMA would avert future "quagmires."

Furthermore, this new style of technowar would rely not on huge, industrial-age armies, but on compact and highly trained formations of select volunteers. Winning wars during the twentieth century had required guts and muscle. Winning wars in the new age just dawning was going to emphasize the seamless blending of technology and skill, while consigning the average citizen to the role of spectator. Fighting promised to remain something other people were paid to do. By extension, this vision of surgical, frictionless, postmodern warfare held the promise of removing constraints that had inhibited the United States in the actual use of its military power. With American society as a whole insulated from the effects of conflict, elites could expect to enjoy greater latitude in deciding when, where, how, and against whom to use force.

Pentagon planners wasted no time in making the RMA the basis for a new American way of war. In 1996, General John Shalikashvili, Powell's successor as JCS chairman, signed off on what the Pentagon chose to style *Joint Vision 2010*, which purported to provide a "conceptual template for how America's Armed Forces will . . . leverage technological opportunities to achieve new levels of effectiveness in joint warfighting."[18]

Considered in retrospect, JV2010 was to the art of war what credit default swaps became to the business of banking: the means to perpetuate a breathtakingly impudent fraud. Yet better than any other single source, that glossy, jargon-laced pamphlet documented the techno-militarism and fevered groupthink to which the officer corps succumbed in the first decade after the Cold War.

JV2010's road map promised to make U.S. forces "persuasive in peace, decisive in war, [and] preeminent in any form of conflict." By exploiting to the fullest the potential of the information revolution, those forces would acquire the ability to defeat any foe anywhere with alacrity and economy. The United States would thereby enjoy "Full-Spectrum Dominance." The text of JV2010 makes the point directly, if not succinctly.

> The combination of these technology trends will provide an order of magnitude improvement in lethality. Commanders will be able to attack targets successfully with fewer platforms and less ordnance while achieving objectives more rapidly and with reduced risk. Individual warfighters will be empowered as never before, with an array of detection, targeting, and communications equipment that will greatly magnify the power of small units.

In sum, by adhering to the formula offered by JV2010, U.S. forces would win quickly and emphatically, always and everywhere, over any adversary large or small, without exception.

Converting this grandiose theory into reality required just two things. First, Congress needed to cough up the necessary funding, expected to be substantial. Second, civilian officials needed to get out of the way and allow military leaders to spend that money as they saw fit. With that, the wonders of full-spectrum dominance would be America's and America's alone, the sole superpower thereby achieving absolute mastery over war itself. Here was militarism laced with Ecstasy.

Free at Last!

The first two elements of the post–Cold War super-story—globalization and militarized global leadership—attracted widespread bipartisan support. Critics on the far left and far right might register complaints about rampant consumerism or express concern about the dangers of incipient militarism. But as is so often the case

with issues related to economic policy or statecraft, those occupying the broad political center outmuscled their adversaries.

In the political mainstream, the vision of a world allowing capitalism free rein with the U.S. military functioning as a sort of
global hall monitor found favor with Democrats and Republicans
alike. Disagreement meant marginalization. Ambitious youngsters
keen to make their mark in Washington knew better than to suggest that the times might be ripe for curbing the nation's appetite
for remaking the world in its own image.

No such agreement existed with respect to the third element
of the post–Cold War super-story, which intruded directly into
the sensitive realm of culture and morality. Its theme was freedom
itself, now expressed in a determination to remove limits on personal
autonomy while discarding restrictions rooted in tradition or religious belief. Here, too, as with globalization and global leadership,
technology had a role to play. Technology offered the tantalizing
prospect of expanding individual choice, even perhaps making it
possible to reinvent human identity and escape the human condition itself. In post–Cold War America, freedom, empowerment,
and choice became all but interchangeable terms.

This push for autonomy reignited long-smoldering divisions in
American society. At the heart of the post–Cold War Kulturkampf
was a dispute over the place of religion in American life. In his book
Culture Wars, published in 1991, the scholar James Davison Hunter
stated the matter crisply. Americans were dividing into two camps.
In the one were those with an "impulse toward orthodoxy," clinging stubbornly to belief in "an external, definable, and transcendent
authority." In the other were those whose "impulse toward progres-
sivism" made them increasingly averse to rules handed down from
on high. In their view, individual empowerment required the
privatization of faith, ending the practice of allowing religiously
derived norms to affect public policy.[19]

Culture warriors on the left, more often than not loosely affiliated with the Democratic Party, saw America as a place in which pervasive discrimination on the basis of race, gender, and sexuality allowed freedom for some—notably for white heterosexual males whose forebears came from northern or western Europe—while denying it to others. They demanded redress of these injustices, with unconditional freedom for all their ultimate goal.

Culture warriors on the right, broadly identified with the Republican Party, believed—indeed, were dead certain—that from its very founding the United States had been the "land of liberty." Yet whether interpreting scripture literally or metaphorically, they took seriously God's warning in Genesis that fateful consequences awaited anyone tempted to reject all limits on the actual exercise of freedom. To disregard that injunction, as had Adam and Eve, was to open the floodgates of moral anarchy. In true freedom, self-restraint tempered self-indulgence.

The dispute—the one side committed to enlarging freedom, the other to insulating it from corruption—allowed little room for compromise or even for reasoned dialogue. The defining feature of America's post–Cold War Kulturkampf was mutual contempt and intolerance. There was no middle ground. Each side charged the other with violating fundamental American values. Neither was immune to partisan manipulation. However much they might disagree on specific details, when it came to promoting global capitalism or preserving American military preeminence, Republicans and Democrats were basically on the same page. When it came to guaranteeing abortion rights or preserving traditional marriage, however, they were on anything but the same page.

Although the struggle to define the true meaning of freedom following the end of history proved exceedingly bitter, it was never a contest between equals. Those advocating the expansion of freedom always enjoyed the upper hand, with defenders of tradition obliged to wage a fighting retreat. On matters related to family, sex, sexuality, and gender, ground lost was lost for good. Cultural conservatives had no difficulty identifying what they were against: decadence, permissiveness, license, and the abandonment of fixed moral standards. When attempting to specify what they were for, however, what they offered seemed indistinguishable from vestigial Puritanism.

As long as the Cold War had lasted, a case could be made for cultivating—or at least aping—Puritanical sternness in the face of evil. Manhattan, Kansas, adjacent to the U.S. Army's Fort Riley, and Manhattan, the borough of New York City, differed in many ways. In both, however, holding Communism at bay meant demonstrating a capacity for sacrifice. Collective acceptance of possible nuclear annihilation pursuant to freedom's defense offered the preeminent symbol of this willingness. In President Kennedy's memorable formulation, to "assure the survival and success of liberty," it was incumbent upon Americans to "pay any price" and "bear any burden." When Kennedy spoke those words, his grandiloquence elicited not guffaws but respectful assent.

Yet "better dead than Red," however gussied up by a skillful wordsmith, worked better as an applause line than as a basis for policy. In practice, even at the height of the Cold War, Americans entertained a limited appetite for bearing burdens, as the conflicts in Korea and Vietnam demonstrated. Vietnam in particular exposed a yawning gap between the emotive posturing of Cold Warriors like JFK and the price that Americans were actually willing to pay.

In that regard, the fall of the Berlin Wall made it unnecessary to prolong what had become over time something of a charade. Prior to 1989, sustaining the pretense of a citizenry standing arm in arm against a common foe, asking what they could do for their country rather than what the country could do for them, retained a certain appeal. After 1989, that was no longer the case.

In effect, the passing of the Cold War relieved Americans of any further obligation to exhibit more than nominal cohesion. Except as a matter of personal preference, virtues such as self-discipline and self-denial, once deemed essential to enabling a nation to stand firm against existential threats, now became passé. The spirit of the post–Cold War era prioritized self-actualization and self-indulgence over self-sacrifice.

None of this happened overnight. Yet incrementally, verities that many, perhaps most, Americans in the immediate aftermath of World War II had found reassuring lost authority, their place taken by a more fluid set of values. As a source of cultural and moral instruction, Boone City eventually took a backseat to Woodstock.

The demise of Communism removed the last remaining constraints on the operation of global capitalism. By leaving the United States militarily preeminent, the end of the Cold War removed any remaining constraints on the use of American coercive power. Similarly, for many ordinary Americans, particularly those of a progressive bent, the passing of the Cold War did away with any lingering constraints on matters related to "lifestyle." No longer would they defer to the customary arbiters of propriety and "good taste" in determining what was permissible and what was not. For transcendent authority, progressives looked to the autonomous self.

To be sure, among freethinkers, the impulse to evade constraints on individual existence long predated the end of the Cold War. Even before the twentieth century, industrialization, urbanization, advances in science, and the transformation of religion from a medium of personal salvation to a means of social uplift had undermined traditional norms. The horrific experience of two successive twentieth-century episodes of total war that saw Western nations obliterating the very concept of moral self-restraint accelerated the process.

In popular memory, the Sixties "changed everything," the triad of sex, drugs, and rock 'n' roll supposedly combining to deep-six the America of Al, Fred, and Homer. Yet while playing to the baby boom generation's sense of self-importance, this interpretation invites exaggeration. On matters relating to race, gender, sex, sexuality, education, expression, and the definition of family, the acids of modernity had for decades been eroding the foundations of the established order. No doubt the sundry commotions associated with the Sixties furthered that process. Yet it was only with the end of the Cold War that the pace of social and cultural change truly kicked into high gear. However impolitic, Patrick Buchanan's notorious 1992 declaration that a culture war was beginning to envelop America was both accurate and timely.

The impact of that metaphorical war was akin to a Category 5 hurricane. The impetus for social and cultural change emanated from the coasts rather than the heartland, from major metropolitan areas rather than lesser towns and cities, and from elite colleges and universities, not factory floors and assembly lines. In the midwestern milieu in which I grew up, the advent of rock and the discovery of pot did not immediately translate into support for social revolution. Arrangements that within a generation would come to be viewed as oppressive, suffocating, and unjust still seemed merely familiar and therefore fixed. I for one lacked the creative imagination to appreciate how quickly such matters would be reclassified as archaic, absurd, or even bigoted.

In the ensuing upheaval, I found myself more a witness than a partisan or participant. During the 1990s, much as had been the case when I was a cadet at West Point watching the events of the 1960s while confined to a quasi-fortress, I did not fully comprehend the forces gathering strength on the other side of the ramparts.

At the center of my incomprehension was the changing status of religion in American life. I was then (and remain today) a believer. As long as the Cold War persisted, religion for me—as for many others—was more than merely an issue of faith. It defined a crucial fault line dividing East and West. They were godless. We were on God's side and He on ours.

The exigencies of the Cold War gave rise to a peculiar form of religiosity that was politically capacious rather than theologically rigorous. Speaking shortly after his election to the presidency in 1952, for example, Dwight D. Eisenhower made the central point. "The great struggle of our times," he said, "is one of spirit. It is a struggle for the hearts and souls of men." The implications were clear: "If we are to be strong we must be strong first in our spiritual convictions." In a famous passage, Ike—himself at best an irregular churchgoer—posited that "our form of government has no sense unless it is founded in a deeply felt religious faith, and I don't care what it is."[20]

Although in some quarters this spiritual Eisenhower Doctrine may have invited derision, Ike's views were congruent with those held by large numbers of ordinary citizens. Within months, the president further embellished this theme. "The churches of America are citadels of our faith in individual freedom and human dignity," he assured a gathering of the National Conference of Christians and Jews. "This faith is the living source of all our spiritual strength. And this strength is our matchless armor in our world-wide struggle against the forces of godless tyranny and oppression."[21]

In short, during the Cold War, religion served as a bulwark of freedom. Once the Cold War ended, however, for many it became something else: an obstacle to freedom's further realization, to be achieved chiefly by lifting constraints on individual autonomy. Indeed, as the Cold War receded into the past, traditional religious observance was to become increasingly associated with ignorance, intolerance, and even fanaticism.

I am not suggesting that Cold War–induced religiosity made Americans more virtuous. Nor do I believe that Eisenhower or any

of his white heterosexual male successors, all of them at least nominally Christian, were better presidents because they attended the
National Prayer Breakfast (instituted in 1953) or participated in
other politico-religious rituals devised during the Cold War.

Yet pressing religion into service as an adjunct to Cold War–era
politics had this secondary effect: It held partially in check inclinations to tamper with institutions (or prohibitions) deriving their
authority from such sources as the Hebrew Bible and the Christian
New Testament. After all, amending the Pledge of Allegiance in
1954 to place the United States "under God" was intended to sig-
nal how "our" side differed from (and was superior to) "theirs."

As the sociologist Will Herberg wrote in his influential book
Protestant, Catholic, Jew, published in 1960, the "Judeo-Christian concept" that found favor during the Cold War expressed "the conviction that at bottom 'the three great faiths' were really 'saying the
same thing' in affirming the 'spiritual ideals' and 'moral values' of
the American Way of Life."[22] As long as the Soviet–American competition continued, anyone questioning the validity of such claims
risked being denounced as unpatriotic.

When the Cold War ended, however, the weight of the argument shifted. While the Pledge underwent no further revision, the
rationale for placing the nation "under God" dissipated. Faith no
longer represented a matchless armor in a worldwide struggle.
Indeed, in the eyes of progressives intent on reimagining freedom
to make it both more expansive and inclusive, religion looked
like an impediment. Unless overturned or amended, its strictures
denied to citizens who were not white, heterosexual, or male rights
and privileges automatically conferred on those who happened to
be just that.

Viewed from this perspective, freedom required the expul-
sion of religion from the public square, with faith thereby reduced
to a private matter and moral deregulation the order of the day.

Henceforth, religion might be tolerated as a personal eccentricity or lifestyle choice, but it was not to play a significant role in public policy. The time had come for God to vacate the premises.

I know of no canonical statement describing the expanded post–Cold War conception of freedom that compares to Friedman's propagandizing on behalf of globalization or *Joint Vision 2010*'s brief in favor of techno-militarism. Even so, leading lights of the American intelligentsia had determined that preserving abortion rights, redefining marriage, ending anti-gay discrimination, dismantling the patriarchy, and promoting multiculturalism now held the keys to creating that "more perfect Union" promised in the Preamble of the Constitution and to securing "the Blessings of Liberty" for all Americans. (Securing equality for people of color had become, at least for a time, less contentious; although racism persisted, like anti-Semitism it had for the moment gone underground.)

Already in the later years of the Cold War, individuals and institutions that fancied themselves summoned to shape the zeitgeist were throwing themselves wholeheartedly behind this cause. In editorial offices of progressive publications, on college and university campuses, throughout the entertainment industry, and among fading mainline Protestant denominations desperately seeking to retain some modicum of relevance—even among image-conscious corporations—maximizing personal choice was emerging as the issue whose time had come.

The end of the Cold War removed God from the picture even as it left Marxism deader than God. With that, autonomy became the summum bonum of the American intelligentsia. To repurpose a phrase dating from when God and Marx were still archrivals, liberating the self now became the "opiate for the intellectuals."[23] As had been the case when priests ruled the roost and when Old Left ideologues declared it self-evident that the future belonged to Communism, contrary opinions were not welcome.

Of course, as the United States embarked upon the post–Cold War era, millions of Americans still clung stubbornly to that Ol' Time Religion or at least went through the motions of doing so. Yet millions of Americans also bowled. That bowling should provide a basis for public policy was an altogether preposterous proposition. Much the same could be said of religion after the end of history.

Demigod in the White House

"The Presidency is the most powerful office in the Free World." So declared John F. Kennedy in 1960 as he announced his intention to run for that office. "In it," he continued, "are centered the hopes of the globe. . . . For it is in the Executive Branch that the most crucial decisions of this century must be made."[24]

However portentous the language, Kennedy was merely restating what most Americans had already come to believe. Since the Great Depression and World War II, but especially as a consequence of the ongoing Cold War, the presidency had become something more than a mere political office with its functions specified in Article II of the U.S. Constitution. Already by 1960, with "the hopes of the globe" centered on a single American called upon to make the century's "most crucial decisions," the presidency had outgrown the Constitution.

Today, with Donald Trump occupying the office that was once Kennedy's, it is useful to recall how, in the decades after World War II, the president became something bigger than a head of government and grander than a chief of state. Entrusted with the authority to order a civilization-obliterating nuclear attack, he served by common consent as "leader of the Free World."

By and large, Americans approved of this development, deeming it necessary and perhaps even fitting. After all, who better than a white heterosexual God-fearing American male to shoulder such awesome responsibilities? Presiding over the West's most powerful nation, the president was, by common consent, the most powerful man anywhere outside the Communist Bloc. The Free World obviously needed a leader. Who but our guy could possibly do the leading?

From time to time, as a matter of courtesy, a president might pretend to acknowledge a coequal, most often a British prime minister able to recite the appropriate lines while reenacting the partnership of Franklin Roosevelt and Winston Churchill. Harold Macmillan served Kennedy in this capacity. Margaret Thatcher did likewise for Ronald Reagan. (After 9/11, Tony Blair revived the role for what is likely to be the last time, his support of George W. Bush's invasion of Iraq prompting unhappy Britons to lampoon their prime minister as the president's "poodle.")[25]

Yet all parties recognized it for the fiction it was. Throughout the Free World, itself a loose and malleable construct, leaders of nations large and small accorded to the president a status that was without equal. Ensuring the cohesion and security of the "West"—a term encompassing nations as culturally non-Western as Japan and South Korea—never formed part of the president's formal job description. Even so, officials from Ottawa to Bonn to Tokyo looked to the occupant of the White House to do just that. For the sake of appearance, the president might play along with the pretense of being primus inter pares. In reality, he was simply primus.

Inherent in the phrase "leader of the Free World" was a large element of chutzpah, akin to Myrtle Beach, South Carolina, declaring itself the "Golf Capital of the World." Yet the trope was not without value. As long as the Cold War continued, here was assurance that there was a captain at the helm, keeping the makeshift vessel SS *Western Civilization* from running aground.

The passing of the Cold War conferred on the president a

further de facto promotion. In place of the misleading but convenient image of a world divided into two opposing camps, there now emerged an equally convenient, even more misleading image of a world dominated by a single superpower, the chief executive of that superpower becoming, in effect, leader of the entire planet.

During the 1992 campaign, Patrick Buchanan had mockingly referred to George H. W. Bush as "the president of the world"—and therefore out of touch with the everyday concerns of ordinary citizens.[26] Yet for many members of the elite, Buchanan's jibe expressed something akin to an expectation. Long since the citadel of national politics, the White House now seemingly became the citadel of global politics. In Washington, the last shreds of reticence and self-awareness disappeared.

So the phrase "leader of the Free World" found a new lease on life, even as the boundaries of that world simultaneously expanded and blurred, with the definition of freedom increasingly becoming a matter of dispute. As more passengers clambered aboard and the SS *Western Civilization* showed signs of becoming less seaworthy, the status and authority of the Helmsman endured. If there was history to be made after the end of history, the president of the United States would make it. So at least many observers, especially members of the American political class, persuaded themselves.

Already by 1960, it had become incumbent upon each president to implement the Cold War bargain, which centered on containing Communism and averting Armageddon. Yet each president gave that consensus his own spin. John Kennedy both understood and welcomed this opportunity, which he immediately embraced. Addressing Congress and the nation in January 1961, barely a week after taking office, he described the circumstances confronting the United States. "Each day we draw nearer the hour of maximum danger," he declared, "as weapons spread and hostile forces grow stronger." The outlook was grim indeed. "I feel I must inform the

Congress," he continued, "that our analyses over the last ten days make it clear that—in each of the principal areas of crisis—the tide of events has been running out and time has not been our friend."[27]

A mere ten days after his inauguration, speaking in an apocalyptic key, Kennedy was asserting a now-established presidential prerogative, issuing a concise but authoritative report about the situation facing the nation. His address offered assurance that he had instantly grasped and was prepared to confront those dangers. Americans could rest easy: Their president was in command of events.

The hour of maximum danger, the tide running out, time not America's friend: Here was the idiom of Cold War politics vividly on display. The words were alarming, verging on hysterical. Yet when uttered by the man who had recently become president, even if by a narrow margin, they acquired instant credibility. Along with his authority to "press the button," here was the great prerogative of Cold War presidents: Past, present, and future were theirs to define.

Not every president did so successfully, of course. Yet for each Ford or Carter, there was a Kennedy or a Reagan, who seemed to vindicate expectations of what presidential leadership could accomplish—even if it did not pay to examine too closely the actual performance of such worthies in office.

From time to time, grumblings about an "imperial presidency" might be heard, usually from someone whose sympathies lay with the party not then controlling the White House.[28] Yet never during the Cold War did this translate into a serious effort to curtail the president's authority or shrink the presidency itself back toward what it had been when Herbert Hoover presided over a White House staff of four.[29]

Nor did the end of the Cold War produce any such curtailment or shrinkage. If anything, the presidency became yet bigger and grander, overshadowing every other aspect of American politics.

After the fall of the Berlin Wall as before, the president was expected to construe and implement the operative political consensus, although one that no longer prioritized opposing Communism and preventing World War III. Those who occupied the Oval Office during the abbreviated post–Cold War era—and those who aspired to the presidency but fell short—differed when it came to specific priorities. But they all promoted globalized neoliberalism and supported militarized hegemony. And whether eagerly or grudgingly, they accommodated themselves to an expanding conception of individual freedom.

Here was the final element of the post–Cold War outlook that defined American politics: a belief that the president of the United States and he alone was called upon to direct history after the end of history.

Unfettered capitalism plus unabashed American global dominion plus the unencumbered self plus visionary, presidential leadership facilitating the fulfillment of those goals: These defined the elements of the post–Cold War consensus propagated by policy intellectuals during the first half of the 1990s. These ideas shaped public discourse much as resisting Communism and defending freedom had shaped public discourse from the late 1940s until the fall of the Berlin Wall.

Yet implicit in this consensus were two notable assumptions: first, that the advantages enjoyed by the United States at the end of the Cold War were insuperable and sure to endure; second, that the great majority of Americans, along with any would-be challengers abroad, would comply with the terms of this consensus, coming to the inescapable realization that no real alternative existed.

Some might gripe and drag their feet, but in the end all would submit. History itself demanded that they do so.

5

BEDFELLOWS

The legitimacy of the presidency and the expectations invested in each president as supreme leader derive from two different sources. The first reflects the nation's democratic ethos. Americans elect their president. His very presence in the White House, therefore, expresses the will of the people, at least in some fashion. That law, custom, the Constitution, and widespread indifference among those eligible to vote may have yielded a less than perfect democracy does not affect the essential verdict: The president is in the White House because We the People put him there.

The second source of presidential legitimacy and of the president's presumed ability to function as global commandant has little to do with democracy. It reflects the oversize influence of elites as gatekeepers in American politics. The United States is formally a democratic republic. In practice, some voices count for much more than others. The self-assigned role of elite institutions in presidential politics is not to decide who will win, but to assess eligibility to compete. The implicit purpose of this vetting process is to exclude would-be candidates deemed unlikely to run the world along lines favored by the Council on Foreign Relations, the Kennedy School of Government, the *Washington Post*, National Public Radio, Wall Street, Silicon Valley, the Israel lobby, the National Rifle Association, the national security apparatus, and mega-donors like the Koch brothers.

Ultimately, the people do choose their president. Yet the choices presented to the people reflect the preferences and interests of a deeply entrenched and supremely self-confident establishment. In voting for president, Americans don't choose between apples and oranges. They choose between two barely distinguishable varieties of apple. Such at least was typically the case until 2016.[1]

That such an arrangement—call it elite-managed democracy—had ostensibly enabled the United States to come out on top in the Cold War all but ensured that it would continue into the post–Cold War era. Why tamper with a system that had delivered the United States to the zenith of global power? The history that Americans chose to remember seemed to show that presidents, taking their cues from the establishment, could indeed direct history.

Yet from the outset this was nonsense on stilts. Allow me to posit an altogether different conception of the president's role from the days of George Washington on. Rather than directing history, presidents generally respond to its imperatives. Rather than setting the course, the Helmsman strives to sense what the winds and currents demand and complies with their apparent dictates.

Of course, some captains are more adept at doing so than others. A successful president correctly discerns what existing conditions require and creates the impression that he is the master of circumstance rather than its servant. James Polk, Abraham Lincoln, and William McKinley offer illustrative examples.

When Polk became president in 1845, pressures to plant the Stars and Stripes on the Pacific coast were becoming intense. Rather than resisting those pressures, he endorsed them. Responding to the putative imperatives of Manifest Destiny, he embarked upon a war of aggression against Mexico that culminated in the annexation of California and much else besides. Thanks to Polk, the United States of America today ranges from sea to shining sea.

In 1861, as Lincoln assumed office, the Union was coming apart. Saving it entailed ending any ambiguity about its purpose. The ensuing Civil War over which he presided destroyed slavery and installed urban industrial capitalism rather than semifeudal agrarianism as the primary basis for organizing society. The United States was soon well on its way to becoming the richest and most dynamic country in the world.

As the nineteenth century was coming to a close, internal pressures on the United States to flex its muscles beyond the confines of North America were growing. Prompted by a restiveness that was economic, geopolitical, and ideological, the urge to expand was once again becoming irresistible. In 1898, McKinley opened the relief valve. During the ensuing war with Spain, the United States helped itself to a maritime empire extending from the Caribbean to the Western Pacific. Thanks to McKinley, in other words, the United States entered the ranks of world powers.

Note that when it came to interpreting winds and currents, the presidents who preceded this trio did not distinguish themselves. During their spell at the helm, John Tyler, James Buchanan, and Grover Cleveland accomplished little of note. As helmsmen, they allowed the country to drift. Predictably, none of the three ranks among presidential greats or near greats.

Nor will Bill Clinton, George W. Bush, and Barack Obama. The three post–Cold War presidents will likely end up ranked alongside Tyler, Buchanan, and Cleveland rather than in the company of Polk, Lincoln, and McKinley.

Clinton, the younger Bush, and Obama were by no means oblivious to what the times seemingly called for. Indeed, whatever their differences in style and temperament, they embodied the over-heated expectations of the Emerald City consensus. Receptive to ideas deemed au courant, salting their speeches with fashionable jargon, and heeding the counsel of well-credentialed advisers, each sought earnestly to comply with its terms.

Yet all three were slow to recognize its defects. Lacking the ability to repair those defects or the imagination to identify an alternative, they unwittingly collaborated in undermining that very consensus. Misreading the winds and misinterpreting the currents, they allowed the ship of state to run aground. Their collective failure paved the way for Donald Trump to take the helm as leader of the Free World.

42 Pries Open the World

Of the three, Bill Clinton was politically the most adept, intellectually the most fecund, and morally the shallowest. If being president is a form of performance art, Clinton demonstrated an astonishing capacity to perform well in just about any environment. Yet that performance came with a dark underside. He was the great chameleon of the post–Cold War interval.

During his eight years in the White House, Clinton vigorously promoted globalization and experimented tentatively with militarized hegemony. He embraced the view, already becoming fashionable, that information technology was changing the nature of both political economy and war, in both cases to American advantage. But to progressives expecting the first baby boom president to lead them to final victory in the culture wars, Clinton proved a disappointment.

Much as had his political idol John F. Kennedy, Clinton took office intent on enshrining his presidency as marking the transition to a new age. In January 1961, Kennedy had proclaimed that, with his inauguration, "the torch has been passed to a new generation of Americans," summoned by Providence to defend freedom "in its hour of maximum danger." In January 1993, Clinton made the same point, albeit in a more upbeat tone. "Today," he declared in his first inaugural address, "a generation raised in the shadows of the cold war assumes new responsibilities in a world warmed by the sunshine of freedom."[2] Like Kennedy, Clinton offered himself as the embodiment of this new age, the hinge on which all else would turn. With conspicuous aplomb, he took it upon himself to explain how Americans might use the sudden burst of sunshine in which they were basking.

Yet as the first president elected in the post–Cold War era, Clinton soon discovered that global primacy implied neither omnipotence nor omniscience. By the standards of American politics, Clinton's qualifies as a successful presidency: By winning a second term in office, he met the basic criterion, one that Jimmy Carter and George H. W. Bush failed to satisfy. Even so, Clinton's legacy includes no signature achievement comparable to the Egypt–Israel peace treaty that Carter negotiated or Bush's management of the Cold War's denouement.

Apart from atmospherics aimed at elite audiences—unveiling a cabinet said to "look like America" and appointing the first female secretary of state—the forty-second president did little to advance the post–Cold War freedom agenda with its emphasis on race, gender, and sexuality. The defining quality of Clinton's approach to cultural issues proved to be risk aversion. He repeatedly proved unwilling to pay any substantial political price to advance causes that he professed to hold close to his heart. When standing up for tolerance and diversity clashed with political expediency, expediency regularly won out.

Typical in that regard was candidate Clinton's well-advertised decision in January 1992 to suspend campaigning so that he could be present in Little Rock for the execution of a mentally impaired black man who, a decade earlier, had murdered a police officer. Ricky Ray Rector needed to die so that Governor Clinton, who otherwise advertised himself as a critic of racism and a strong advocate for the mentally ill, could assure voters that as president he would be tough on crime.[3]

Rector's execution would hardly be the last time in Clinton's career that political calculations overrode principle. A tendency to abandon or distance himself from ostensibly cherished values when they became politically inconvenient was to become a hallmark of his presidency. For example, candidate Clinton had promised if elected to issue an executive order allowing gays to serve in the military. Yet in the very first days of his presidency, facing concerted opposition from the Joint Chiefs of Staff, to include JCS Chairman Colin Powell, he abandoned that promise. Confronting the prospect of insisting that senior military leaders obey his orders as they were sworn to do, the commander in chief beat a hasty retreat.

A comparable episode occurred in 1996 when the Defense of Marriage Act landed on Clinton's desk for signature. Large majorities in both houses of Congress had voted in favor of this legislation, which officially defined marriage as "a legal union between one man and one woman as husband and wife." Clinton might, as a statement of principle, have vetoed the legislation, even knowing that Congress was likely to override that veto. Instead, up for reelection that year, he signed it. For gays who numbered among his most fervent supporters, this amounted to outright betrayal.

In truth, Bill Clinton was ill-suited to the role of supplanting white heteronormative patriarchy with a more inclusive and accommodating conception of freedom. Although he posed as a cultural progressive, the fit was awkward indeed. Beset by rumors of serial infidelity even prior to becoming president, he carried way too much personal baggage to have any credibility as a critic of the existing order. Lurid revelations of Clinton's affair with a White

House intern seemingly confirmed what many already suspected: Here was someone less interested in transcending patriarchy than availing himself of its privileges.

That said, in any fair-minded evaluation of the Clinton presidency, Monica Lewinsky should count for considerably less than, say, Carlos Salinas de Gortari or Slobodan Milošević. As president of Mexico, the now largely forgotten Salinas partnered with Clinton in closing the deal that produced the North American Free Trade Agreement. The Serb nationalist Milošević, Clinton's chief nemesis during the decade-long disintegration of Yugoslavia touched off by the collapse of Communism, offered the president a chance to prove his chops as wartime commander in chief.

Clinton saw NAFTA as an opportunity to validate neoliberal precepts and attach a booster rocket to globalization. It offered Americans "the chance to do what our parents did before us." So the president explained in December 1993 as he made the partnership official. "We have the opportunity to remake the world," he contended, by instituting a new economic order "that will promote more growth, more equality, better preservation of the environment, and a greater possibility of world peace."

Yet implicit in his remarks was an admission that the actual role of the United States was less to remake than to comply. "We cannot stop global change," he continued.

We cannot repeal the international economic competition that is everywhere. We can only harness the energy to our benefit. Now we must recognize that the only way for a wealthy nation to grow richer is to export, to simply find new customers for the products and services it makes.

Embracing this reality, Clinton insisted, would benefit all Americans. "For two decades, most people have worked harder for less.

Seemingly secure jobs have been lost." Now, he promised, that would begin to change. "When I affix my signature to the NAFTA legislation a few moments from now," he concluded, "I do so with this pledge:

> To the men and women of our country who were afraid of these changes and found in their opposition to NAFTA an expression of that fear—what I thought was a wrong expression and what I know was a wrong expression but nonetheless represented legitimate fears—the gains from this agreement will be your gains, too.[4]

Here was a forthright explanation of what the average American could expect by conforming to, rather than vainly resisting, the forces of globalization: Things were going to get better for everyone. Yet embedded in this promise was a tacit presidential admission that by joining NAFTA the United States was doing what circumstances obliged it to do.

Compliance with the dictates of globalization was not a voluntary proposition. Assessing the nation's situation from his post atop the bridge, the Helmsman could see no alternative to the altered course he was setting. Yet under the terms of the post–Cold War consensus, which anointed the U.S. president as global leader, it was incumbent upon Clinton to sustain the pretense that the choice was actually his. Doing so, of course, would position him to claim credit for the benefits that globalization was expected to yield.

NAFTA helped pave the way for many other Clinton-era initiatives intended to enhance economic openness. The most important of these were offering China most-favored-nation trade status in 1993 and joining the newly created World Trade Organization in 1995. Equally noteworthy, however, were a series of measures touted as positioning the United States to compete more effectively in a globalizing economy.

Prominent among these measures was the repeal of the Glass-Steagall Act of 1933. A response to the financial chicanery that had contributed to the Great Depression, Glass-Steagall had governed the American banking industry for decades. During that period, Clinton conceded, it had "worked pretty well for the industrial economy," which the president characterized as "highly organized," centralized, and national. But in the wake of the Cold War, that economy was fast disappearing. Replacing Glass-Steagall, he gushed, was "the most important recent example of our efforts here in Washington to maximize the possibilities of the new information age global economy." In that regard, the Financial Services Modernization Act of 1999, which he signed with marked enthusiasm, held the key to "modernizing the financial services industry, tearing down these antiquated walls, and granting banks significant new authority." Yet in typically Clintonesque fashion, the president hastened to add that the new banking regime would also "save consumers billions of dollars a year" and "protect the rights of consumers." Not surprisingly, investment bankers, including those occupying senior positions in his administration, and those members of Congress who specialized in serving the interests of Wall Street, applauded.[5]

Globalization provoked opposition, as change in any form typically does. Yet critics found themselves at a disadvantage. While they might object to the apparent commodification of everything, they could not explain how repealing or reversing trends toward economic integration would improve human well-being. As populations grew, so did demands for food, clothing, shelter, and diversion. The creation of a new global order that was both open and seamlessly connected held the prospect of satisfying those demands. To suggest that globalization-induced uniformity, homogenization, and specialization were too high a price to pay was tantamount to arguing in favor of self-abnegation and austerity. Except perhaps in monastic communities, such virtues evoked little enthusiasm among Americans as the twentieth century was winding down.

As with NAFTA, so, too, with U.S. armed intervention in the Balkans: Here, again, even if hesitantly, Clinton concluded that circumstances dictated a specific response. Given the immensity of the humanitarian catastrophe triggered by the disintegration of the former Yugoslavia, inaction became tantamount to complicity. So as with globalization, the United States, despite its preponderant power, somehow found itself without any real choice. It had to act. Only with time would the adverse implications of action become clear. Unknowingly, Clinton was nudging the United States down a path toward permanent war, with the eventual loss of American preponderance one result.

The Balkan crisis of the 1990s culminated in two brief U.S.-orchestrated bombing campaigns, first in Bosnia and then in Kosovo. Following each came a protracted U.S.-led military occupation. In an immediate sense, intervention produced the intended political payoff. Slobodan Milošević's efforts to create an ethnically pure Greater Serbia failed. The upheaval that he had done so much to instigate subsided. The Serb leader ended his days in the dock at the International Criminal Court in The Hague.

From the Clinton administration's perspective and that of national security experts more generally, the confrontation with Milošević yielded three distinct conclusions. First, it revealed the pusillanimity of America's European allies, who proved unable to stem the barbarism engulfing parts of the former Yugoslavia as that country came apart. Second, it exposed the weakness of post–Soviet Russia, which lacked the muscle to fulfill its self-assigned role as protector of the Slavs. And finally it demonstrated the feasibility of relying on military action to enforce norms and punish bad behavior, almost without cost to U.S. forces, an approach with obvious potential for application elsewhere.

The first of those conclusions turned out to be accurate, as did the second, although Russian tolerance for being pushed around would prove short-lived. As for the third and most important: It was to become a source of lasting grief for the United States and others. According to President Clinton, "The success of the air campaign in Kosovo marked a new chapter in military history."[6] Unfortunately, history itself quickly overturned that judgment.

In the ceaselessly updated chronicle of the American military experience, the Bosnia and Kosovo campaigns—Operation Deliberate Force, lasting just three weeks in the late summer of 1995, and Operation Allied Force, spread across seventy-eight days in the spring of 1999—have long since been crowded out. Both featured what military theorists were then calling "precision bombing." In both cases, American air forces operated at high altitudes and faced negligible resistance, with U.S. losses all but nonexistent.

In comparison with Korea and Vietnam or with the conflicts that followed in the wake of 9/11, these abbreviated Balkan campaigns qualify as trivial by almost any measure: duration, cost, ordnance expended, or casualties inflicted and sustained. Yet during Clinton's eight-year tenure as commander in chief, these were the only victories the U.S. military was able to claim. As such, at least for a time, they shaped American expectations regarding the use of force. Here, it seemed, was evidence that the United States had solved the riddle of making armed might politically purposeful. Full-Spectrum Dominance was no longer a theory. Bosnia and Kosovo made it fact.

Yet categorizing the Balkan interventions as significant successes provided an excuse to avoid serious reflection on the broader post–Cold War pattern of military activism that Clinton did much to promote. In the Balkans, U.S. forces seemingly demonstrated an ability to accomplish the assigned mission, quickly and decisively. Elsewhere, however, the outcomes achieved on Clinton's watch appeared far more ambiguous. Intervention in Somalia, for instance, ended in abject failure after the notorious Blackhawk Down firefight of October 1993. While Operation Uphold Democracy in 1994 ousted the military junta that had ruled Haiti, it produced negligible benefits for the people of that impoverished country.

Clinton's support for NATO's eastward expansion to Russia's very borders persuaded Kremlin leaders that Washington's intentions were anything but benign, even as American-devised schemes for "shock therapy" were playing havoc with the post–Soviet Russian economy.[7] As for his response to Osama bin Laden's 1996 "Declaration of Jihad against the Americans Occupying the Land of the Two Holy Mosques," it was, to put it mildly, ineffective.[8] A similar judgment applies to the recurring air strikes conducted on the president's order that dropped hundreds of munitions on targets in Iraq, Afghanistan, and Sudan. Apart from providing a rationale for replenishing U.S. weapons stocks, they accomplished next to nothing.

In retrospect, NAFTA (subsequently discredited and scrapped) and the small wars in the Balkans (soon forgotten) capture the essential elements of Clinton's legacy: the promotion of economic openness and integration along with a growing penchant for military interventionism, both buoyed by Clinton's faith in the transformative potential of technology.

Clinton himself would disagree, of course. Indeed, anyone willing to wade through his 957-page memoir will encounter a different interpretation of his presidency. Excruciatingly detailed and nominally comprehensive (even while avoiding any mention of Ricky Ray Rector or the Defense of Marriage Act), *My Life* conveys a sense of Clinton's personal energy and exuberance, his delight in wielding power, his remarkable capacity for mastering the details of policy, and his acute sensitivity to personal criticism.

Ever the policy guru, Clinton uses that memoir to explain in laborious detail his administration's efforts to reform the nation's health-care system, which failed, his endorsement of the Oslo Peace Accords, which did not bring peace, and his success in balancing the budget, which did not outlast his time in office. As for Clinton's decision to scrap the existing welfare system, his crackdown on crime, and his support for NATO expansion, all of which at the time seemed like a big deal, each produced unintended and unwelcome consequences.

From our present perspective, policy initiatives undertaken with great fanfare in the 1990s have faded into insignificance. As for Clinton's summary assessment of his presidency, it simply won't wash. "Life got better for all Americans," he wrote of his eight years as president, and "we brought more hope for peace, freedom, security, and prosperity to people all over the world."[9] That conclusion raised eyebrows when it appeared in 2004. Today, it invites derision.

A more accurate summary judgment might go like this: By the time Bill Clinton retired from office and headed for the bright lights of Manhattan rather than back to Little Rock, the patriarchy remained firmly in place. With hardly more than token exceptions, white males still ruled the roost in Washington, on Wall Street, in Hollywood, and in just about every other quarter of American life where there was power to wield and money to be made. Gays could neither marry nor serve openly in the U.S. military. On the freedom front, in other words, Clinton's substantive accomplishments were meager.

Yet on matters relating to war, Clinton left an indelible mark. He routinized the use of force, thereby furthering the militarization of American global leadership. Having himself avoided service in Vietnam, he helped his countrymen shed the aversion to war induced by that conflict. In 1991, when U.S. forces set out to liberate Kuwait, Americans had held their breath, fearful that some disaster might befall the troops, with the nation sucked into a new quagmire. Over the course of Clinton's presidency, such fears abated and Americans learned to take war in stride. Observing from a safe distance, they became comfortable with war.

At least as significantly, during his eight years in office, checks on American-style corporate capitalism all but disappeared. Deference to the dictates of openness and the imperatives of interconnectedness became all but mandatory. On that score, globalization had no firmer friend than the forty-second president.

Whether Clinton's overall legacy would prove beneficial to the American people remained to be seen. I had my doubts. As a former soldier and a student of history, I was left uneasy by the post–Cold War predilection for using force. As for technology enhancing war's utility, that struck me as a proposition fraught with hazard. In my new identity as a middle-aged academic novice of conservative bent, moreover, I found the hype surrounding globalization difficult to distinguish from old-fashioned greed. Did "more" and "faster" really offer the keys to human happiness? Was planet Earth capable of tolerating the stress to which it was subjected by runaway capitalism? I saw little reason to think so.

We may state with confidence that Donald Trump spent little time pondering such questions. During the Clinton era, he remained a celebrity of sorts and a symbol of excess, but also the butt of jokes. (In a 1993 *Washington Post* "Style Invitational," the fifth runner-up prize went to the author of this witticism: "Donald Trump is so annoying that Amnesty International wants him beaten and locked up.")[10] Yet as the end of the decade (and of the Clinton presidency) approached, Trump toyed with making a run for the White House himself. "I would be a great president," he declared.[11]

To spell out his platform, Trump even published a book reassuringly titled *The America We Deserve*.[12] In its introduction, Trump promised "straight talk about politics." In fact, the text combined large promises—"I have a plan to pay off the national debt entirely, cut taxes for the middle class, repeal the inheritance tax, and save Social Security"—with notably small-bore proposals, few of them original. The overall tone was immodest. It was, in short, a typical political tract.

As his political model, Trump cited Wendell Willkie, the business executive who in 1940 captured the Republican presidential nomination, only to be defeated in the general election by Franklin Roosevelt. Willkie was a centrist, as was the circa 2000 version of Donald Trump.

In *The America We Deserve*, Trump came out in favor of safe streets, safe schools, new schools, and school choice. He opposed discrimination, whether based on race, gender, or sexual orientation. He was pro-choice, but would prohibit partial birth abortions. He supported gun rights, but also a ban on assault weapons. To get ahead of crime, he advocated "proactive" policing. To promote economic growth, he proposed cutting taxes, cutting bureaucracy, and cutting burdensome regulations. On health care, he endorsed a variant of Canada's single-payer system.

The longest, and for our purposes, most instructive chapter in *The America We Deserve* dealt with foreign policy. Its overarching theme was pragmatism. "The day of the chess player is over," Trump wrote (or paid someone to write). "American foreign policy has to be put in the hands of a dealmaker." Here his models were Franklin Roosevelt and Richard Nixon (both of whom, in fact, saw statecraft as akin to chess). Trump depicted himself as neither an isolationist nor a "giddy globalist." He put himself somewhere in the middle. "The key is prudence," he observed, "just the right balance of idealism and practical good sense."

In practice, this meant casting a wary eye toward China.

Economic ties with that rising Asian superpower should not require the United States to "trade away our principles," wrote Trump, professing particular concern for "the mistreatment of China's citizens by their own government." After China, North Korea posed the "biggest menace" to U.S. security. To forestall the possibility of North Korea acquiring nuclear weapons, he proposed a "surgical strike," that action sending a "message around the world that the United States is going to eliminate any serious threat to its security, and do so without apology." Trump hinted that limited military action targeting Iraq and Iran might also be in order. He also promised to get tough on Russia—"if they want our dime, they had better do our dance"—and to indict Fidel Castro on charges of murder and terrorism. His views on immigration were then still tepid. "Let's be extremely careful not to admit more people than we can absorb" was all he had to say. There was no mention of border walls, no proposed mass expulsions, and no slurs directed at particular ethnic groups. As to terrorism, with 9/11 still in the future, it was the homegrown variety that worried him. "The biggest threat to our security is ourselves," he wrote. Like just about everyone else in American politics, he called for increased military spending and made clear his support for Israel. "We have been there for Israel," he wrote, "because Israel is there for us."

In television interviews, untethered from his ghostwriter, the all-but-official candidate repeated his promise to boost economic growth and wipe out the national debt. He also vowed to press ahead with Ronald Reagan's proposed "Star Wars" ballistic missile defenses. His big dream was "cleaning up the world from nuclear missiles." That would be "nirvana," he said. And although planning to run as the candidate of the short-lived Reform Party, he expected "construction workers [and] taxicab drivers" to rally to his cause. He was for the little guy. "Rich people don't like me," he explained. Yet apart from his stated intention to "tax people of wealth," and his support for abortion, Trump's positions did not differ substantially from those of the Republican Party.[13] As to where exactly post–Cold War America might be headed, he had almost nothing to say.

For that very reason, his decision to withdraw from the race in February 2000 did not come as a surprise. Trump had not yet figured out how to position himself as a richer-than-Croesus enemy of the establishment. Nor was the moment ripe for a faux-populist. That said, an aversion to mixing with the hoi polloi might also have given him second thoughts. "I'm not a fan of the handshake. I think it's barbaric," he confessed. "Shaking hands, you catch colds, you catch the flu, you catch this, you catch all sorts of things."[14] For now, Trump would bide his time.

43 Goes for Broke

Has George W. Bush ever wondered what course his presidency might have followed had 9/11 not occurred? Surely, he must have.

Reeling from the shock of the attack on the World Trade Center and the Pentagon, more than a few observers took to referring to September 11, 2001, as the date that "changed everything." This turned out not to be the case. Yet the events of that day surely changed our forty-third president, profoundly and irrevocably. As a candidate for high office, Bush had presented himself as an exponent of "compassionate conservatism," sensitive to the plight of those in need.[15] He had advocated a "humble" approach to foreign policy, remarking, "I'm not so sure the role of the United States is going around the world saying this is the way it's gotta be."[16] A pushy America was more likely to foster antagonism than win friends, he believed.

As it is, we will never know with certainty how Bush might have translated such inclinations into policy. On 9/11, Mohamed Atta and his eighteen coconspirators not only took the controls of four American passenger jets, they all but commandeered the Bush presidency. Bush himself emerged from what he called the "day of fire" as the spiritual heir of Woodrow Wilson, perhaps the least humble president since the founding of the Republic.

Early in the prior century, President Wilson had taken it upon himself to propose a "new international order under which reason and justice and the common interests of mankind shall prevail."[17] He vowed to end the scourge of war, to teach other countries "to elect good men," and to make the world itself "safe for democracy." Wilson had come to these positions incrementally over time, prodded by a series of crises abroad. After 9/11, comparably ambitious aspirations seized George W. Bush in a matter of days. He promptly proceeded to out-Wilson Wilson. It was a remarkable transformation.

In terms of style and personality, Bush was the polar opposite of his predecessor. Whereas Clinton had been a fast starter, Bush was a late bloomer. As a young man, this son of privilege appeared bound for anything but glory. Like his father, he played baseball at Yale and made Skull and Bones, while graduating without distinction. Unlike his father, when the opportunity to go to war presented itself, he passed. Yet as the younger Bush matured, decency, amiability, and a becoming folksiness, these not unconnected to a newfound personal religiosity, emerged as defining traits.

In 1932, the journalist Walter Lippmann had waspishly pronounced New York governor Franklin Roosevelt "a pleasant man who, without any important qualifications for the office, would very much like to be President."[18] The description far more accurately fits Texas governor George W. Bush in 2000. Lippmann had underestimated Roosevelt, who once in office demonstrated an uncanny ability to rise to any occasion. After September 11, 2001, with a calamity surpassing that of December 7, 1941, fate summoned Bush to emulate Roosevelt's greatness. Although his basic decency and amiability persisted, modesty was gone for good. As had been the case with Wilson, so it proved with Bush: As challenges mounted, wisdom and prudence dissipated.

Of course, in a sense, Roosevelt had it easy: Knowing who the enemy was—Hitler helped by declaring war on the United States just days after Pearl Harbor—made the problem of defining objectives, devising strategies, and sustaining domestic support somewhat more manageable. Although Bush wasted no time after 9/11 in concluding that the nation was at war, deciding who or what we were fighting, much less identifying the war's purpose, proved more elusive. The president's prior experience had ill-prepared him to address such matters and made him subject to manipulation.

Culturally, Bush was a Boone City kind of guy who took office in what was well on its way to becoming an Emerald City moment. Little evidence exists to suggest that the forty-third president was himself overtly racist, sexist, or homophobic. Yet neither did he view the extirpation of racism, sexism, and homophobia as a priority. His conception of individual freedom fixed in place by his religious convictions, Bush wasted no energy trying to revise its boundaries.

On matters of political economy, Bush by and large hewed to the neoliberal course that Clinton had set. He favored free trade, low taxes, and easing restrictions on business activity, while reciting the standard GOP line on fiscal discipline. Impeding the U.S.-led march toward an open and integrated world did not form part of his agenda. And in the tradition of Ronald Reagan, he vowed to rebuild a military establishment that a Democratic administration had purportedly kept on half rations and treated with disrespect.

Bush the outdoorsman appreciated clean air, clean water, and wide-open spaces. But on matters related to the environment, he was a traditionalist and therefore a climate-change skeptic. The devastation caused by Hurricane Katrina, to which his administration responded with unmitigated incompetence, did not substantially alter his views. Yet his was not a do-nothing presidency. He sought to reform public education and improve health care, even if results achieved fell well short of those promised.

So Bush's overall record was not devoid of accomplishment. Yet little of what he did domestically matters. In the end, actions at home, even when worthy, no more redeemed Bush's presidency than did supporting a federal antilynching law redeem the hapless Warren G. Harding's in the 1920s.

The central theme of Bill Clinton's tenure in office had been globalization. The central theme of George W. Bush's tenure became war, which some in his administration conceived as a sort of complement to globalization—another approach to bringing the world into conformity with American preferences. While Clinton had dabbled in war, the events of September 11 prompted Bush to embrace it wholeheartedly. Wars that still today follow their meandering course ultimately consumed his presidency.

The name devised to justify those conflicts—the Global War on Terrorism—amounted to an exercise in misdirection. The horrors of 9/11 notwithstanding, terrorism does not pose an existential threat to the United States and never has. As innumerable commentators have noted, terrorism is merely a tactic, and an ancient one at that, employed in support of worthy purposes, as well as nefarious ones. As an explanation for U.S. policy after 9/11, terrorism comes nowhere near to being adequate. Indeed, much like the shelling of Fort Sumter in 1861 or the sinking of the USS *Maine* in 1898, the attack on the World Trade Center and the Pentagon served less as a proximate cause for war than as a catalyst.

In truth, several factors caused this war. One stands out as particularly relevant to this account: a combustible form of American Exceptionalism that formed after the end of the Cold War but remained largely dormant until Osama bin Laden provided the necessary detonator.

Of course, a conviction that God has bestowed on the United States unique prerogatives is deeply embedded in the nation's collective consciousness. Yet this particular variant of American Exceptionalism incorporated three distinctive themes: unvarnished militarism, missionary zealotry, and extreme nationalism. Prior American experience had offered glimpses of each. Distinguishing this particular recurrence was the chain reaction they produced as they came together.

That said, the events that ensued were not entirely George Bush's doing. After all, the Bush who took office in January 2001 was neither a militarist nor a zealot nor a rabid nationalist. Yet within his administration each of the impulses found a champion who, at least for a time, had the president's ear.

To run the Pentagon, Bush recruited a militarist, Donald Rumsfeld. To serve as Rumsfeld's deputy, he appointed a zealot, Paul Wolfowitz. As his own running mate, he chose an arch nationalist, Richard Cheney. None of these three members of the American elite, each bearing credentials more impressive than the president himself, lacked self-confidence or political acuity. Each had already demonstrated a well-honed aptitude for fearmongering. They were, to use a term coined by the historian Jacob Burckhardt, "emergency men."[19] Only when personally engaged in deflecting some dire threat to the nation (or the planet) did they come fully alive.

Sidelined during the years of the Clinton presidency, each member of this unholy trinity had roundly criticized Clinton for lacking assertiveness. Each hankered to put American power to work, not in pursuit of small purposes but very large ones indeed. For each, the events of 9/11 suggested the possibility of doing just that, not merely bringing the perpetrators of the attack to justice—that qualified as incidental—but securing permanent and unambiguous American global dominance, all under the guise of spreading freedom and punishing evildoers. If an epic calamity, therefore, 9/11 was also an opportunity, one that Rumsfeld, Wolfowitz, and Cheney had no intention of wasting. Mere hours after the attack on the Pentagon, the defense secretary was already sketching out a plan of action: major war to achieve major objectives. "Go massive," he directed his aides. "Sweep it all up. Things related and not."[20]

None of this is to suggest that Bush served as a mere mouthpiece or puppet. He was, by his own account, fully in charge. As he once put it, "I'm the decider, and I decide what's best."[21] Yet had Bush chosen to look elsewhere for counsel—to his more circumspect father, for example—things might have gone differently.

As it was, to kick-start his war, the decider decided to invade Afghanistan in the fall of 2001 and then Iraq in the spring of 2003. The immediate aim of the former, known as Operation Enduring Freedom, was to overthrow the Taliban, guilty of having provided sanctuary to Osama bin Laden and members of al-Qaeda. The immediate purpose of the latter, known as Operation Iraqi Freedom, was to topple Saddam Hussein, accused of possessing weapons of mass destruction and being in cahoots with bin Laden.

Yet immediate or advertised purpose does not describe actual purpose. As measured by the number of U.S. troops committed to these two campaigns, they do not qualify for inclusion in the roster of America's truly big wars. Yet their underlying purpose was revolutionary. Together they were to provide a springboard for a sweeping reconfiguration of basic national security policy. Rumsfeld counted on these wars to demonstrate beyond the shadow of a doubt that the United States was now top dog militarily and would be for decades to come. For Wolfowitz, Enduring Freedom and Iraqi Freedom would demonstrate the willingness, even eagerness, of the United States to remove regimes of which it disapproved and its capacity to install in their stead governments devoted to liberal democratic values. For Cheney, decisive victories in Afghanistan and Iraq, gained rapidly and economically, would provide an object lesson regarding the fate awaiting any nation or entity having the temerity to defy U.S. demands.

Here was turn-of-the-twentieth-century American imperialism revived, reinforced, and rebranded under the label Freedom Agenda. Rumsfeld, Wolfowitz, and Cheney saw in war the means to remove any last doubts about who was calling the shots on planet Earth. The ambitions they entertained were without limits.

Yet it fell to the president himself to translate these grandiose ambitions into a coherent framework for policy. This he did in a series of notable statements and documents, beginning with his initial response to 9/11 and culminating in his second inaugural address. The younger Bush thereby accomplished something that his father had failed to do: With verve, conviction, and surprising eloquence, he articulated the basis for a new world order, Made in the USA, directed from Washington, and enforced by American military muscle.

Of course, events have long since exposed the defects in the position Bush staked out, much as events in the aftermath of World War I exposed the naïveté and fallacies of the order that Woodrow Wilson had proposed in his famous Fourteen Points. Yet when first unveiled, Wilson's plan for peace had generated enthusiastic applause: Here was a blueprint for the way the world was supposed to work. As such, even today the Fourteen Points merit a prominent place in the national catalog of great state papers.

So do the documents in which George W. Bush spelled out the terms of his own new world order. Given the myriad adverse consequences to which it gave birth, Bush's vision of peace-through-dominion has long since ceased to engender applause. For the very reason that it once formed the basis of U.S. policy, however, that discredited vision merits careful reflection.

As prime minister of France in World War I, Georges Clemenceau had wondered why Wilson needed Fourteen Points when God had contented himself with just Ten Commandments. Bush outdid both Wilson and the Lord, limiting himself to a mere Five Propositions.

First, America's purposes are beyond reproach. Speaking to Congress just nine days after 9/11, Bush addressed the question he believed was on the minds of many: "Why do they hate us?" He had an answer readily at hand. "They hate our freedoms—our freedom of religion, our freedom of speech, our freedom to vote and assemble and disagree with each other," the president declared.[22] That prior U.S. actions might have fueled animosity leading to terrorism was not something he was prepared to consider. Events that predated 9/11, whether by a year or a century, were without relevance.

Second, viable alternatives to the principles defining the American way of life do not exist. In a commencement address to graduating cadets at West Point in June 2002, the president restated and endorsed Fukuyama's thesis: The American present defined the world's future. "The 20th century ended with a single surviving model of human progress," he asserted, "based on non-negotiable demands of human dignity, the rule of law, limits on the power of the state, respect for women and private property and free speech and equal justice and religious tolerance."[23] American values are universal values; compliance is therefore compulsory and resistance futile.

Third, when forced to fight, the United States wages war on behalf of righteousness itself. "Wherever we carry it," Bush told the graduating cadets, "the American flag will stand not only for our power, but for freedom. Our nation's cause has always been larger than our nation's defense. We fight, as we always fight, for a just peace—a peace that favors human liberty. We will defend the peace against threats from terrorists and tyrants. We will preserve the peace by building good relations among the great powers. And we will extend the peace by encouraging free and open societies on every continent."

Fourth, each of the first three propositions confers on the United States unique prerogatives as self-assigned global peace enforcer. "For much of the last century," Bush acknowledged, "America's defense relied on the Cold War doctrines of deterrence and containment." The events of 9/11 had made those concepts obsolete. New threats required "new thinking." The times called for activism. The war on terror would "not be won on the defensive." It was incumbent upon the United States to "take the battle to the enemy, disrupt his plans, and confront the worst threats before they emerge. In the world we have entered, the only path to safety is the path of action. And this nation will act." The United States thereby arrogated to itself the authority to designate certain regimes as "evil" and to wage preventive war to destroy them. International law had hitherto condemned preventive war, the Nuremberg tribunal calling it the "supreme crime." Bush now exempted the United States from such prohibitions.

Fifth, the ultimate triumph of this American-constructed new world order is foreordained. "I know there are struggles ahead, and dangers to face," Bush acknowledged. "But this country will define our times, not be defined by them. As long as the United States of America is determined and strong, this will not be an age of terror; this will be an age of liberty, here and across the world."[24] On a later occasion, he put it this way: "By our efforts, we have lit a fire . . . in the minds of men. It warms those who feel its power, it burns those who fight its progress, and one day this untamed fire of freedom will reach the darkest corners of our world."[25] Such freedom, backed by the world's best military, was unstoppable. War itself would provide the means to ratify America's role as the engine of history.

Together these five propositions comprised not simply a Bush Doctrine, but a Bush Eschatology. Investing the president with the authority to make such grand claims was a codicil known as the theory of the unitary executive.[26] Exploited by administration lawyers, this theory became, in effect, a sixth proposition. It bestowed on the president the equivalent of papal authority to pronounce upon the meaning and purpose of existence, while simultaneously empowering him to do what the pope can no longer do: dispatch his legions to enforce his will wherever and however he should see fit. The theory of the unitary executive exalted Bush as both philosopher-king and generalissimo. All that was needed to validate such claims was for the Global War on Terrorism to follow the course envisioned by Rumsfeld, Wolfowitz, and Cheney. This, of course, was not to be.

The Bush Eschatology struck me even then as vainglorious, if not altogether blasphemous. Yet by no means did it signify a fundamental change in the trajectory of post–Cold War American statecraft. On the contrary, it reaffirmed in the strongest possible terms the premises underlying those policies.

What had been implicit now became explicit. What Fukuyama had posited as theory, Bush now declared to be reality. To my mind, well before September 2001, U.S. policy had shown worrisome signs of becoming unhinged. Now it went altogether off the rails. Yet the problem, as I saw it, was not Bush. Nor was it Rumsfeld, Wolfowitz, and Cheney. It was the mindset that they and others of their ilk had absorbed and with it a preference for myth over reality, especially when it came to their own country and its past.

So I did what academics do. I published books, wrote op-eds, lectured, and responded to media inquiries. In that regard, the Bush era was not without its rewards. My phone rang more frequently. Invitations arrived.

Although I persisted in identifying myself as a conservative, my critique of U.S. policy struck a chord on the left. My minuscule fan base consisted largely of well-educated and well-informed baby boomers, many of whom had cut their political eyeteeth opposing the war in which I had participated. My interaction with these progressives was invariably pleasant and even touching. They were genuine idealists. In their ranks, the hopes and aspirations of the 1960s lived on. Yet in post–Cold War America, their actual influence was negligible. Their political irrelevance hinted at the fate of the critique I was fashioning.

That said, various senators, representatives, and other personages— eventually even one president of the United States—solicited my views. All made a polite show of interest in what I had to say. From time to time, I trooped down to Washington to testify before some congressional committee. And on a few occasions, I appeared on national news programs, typically as a sort of foil for guests spouting establishment views.

Virtually all of this was theater, as I soon came to realize. I had inadvertently become a minor player in what was the political equivalent of a Potemkin village, pretending to debate matters that were not in actuality up for discussion. All the chatter served one purpose only: It distracted attention from the shackles imposed by what passed for conventional wisdom.

As for Donald Trump, he was now commanding a far wider audience. During the Bush era, he prospered and became a major media presence, treated as both laughingstock and sage. In April 2004, he even hosted *Saturday Night Live*, one of the nation's highest accolades. "Nobody's bigger than me, nobody's better than me," he bragged after the show. "I'm a ratings machine."[27] In a sense, he was. Not surprisingly, ratings-conscious news networks and radio talk show hosts regularly booked him, not to discuss real estate deals or gambling casinos, but to get his views on the leading public policy controversies of the day.

Trump was nothing if not opinionated. Whether his opinions reflected an accurate understanding of any particular situation was beside the point. He himself shared the media's preoccupation with "newsmakers," playing to the notion that the words and actions of particularly prominent individuals shape reality rather than the reverse. Put in front of a microphone, Trump could always be counted to express strong opinions. He was good copy. To the news organizations serving as his fawning enablers, this defined Trump's value.

Here, for example, are extracts of an interview Wolf Blitzer did with Trump in March 2007 for CNN's *The Situation Room.*[28]

BLITZER: The [Iraq] war is hovering over politics right now, as it should. . . . Give us your assessment. Is there a way out?

TRUMP: The war is a total disaster. It's a catastrophe, nothing less. It is such a shame that this took place. In fact, I gained a lot of respect for our current president's father by the fact that he had the sense not to go into Iraq. He won the war and then said, Let's not go the rest of the way. And he turned out to be right. And Saddam Hussein, whether they liked him or didn't like him, he hated terrorists. He'd shoot and kill terrorists. When terrorists came into his country, which he did control and he did dominate, he would kill terrorists. Now it's a breeding ground for terrorists. So, look, the war is a total catastrophe.

BLITZER: Who do you blame?

TRUMP: Well, there's only one person you can blame, and that's our current president. I mean, obviously Rumsfeld was a disaster, and other people that are giving him advice have been a disaster. And Condoleezza Rice, who's a lovely woman, but she never makes a deal—she doesn't make deals, she waves. She gets off the plane, she waves, she sits down with some dictator—forty-five-degree angle, they do the camera shot. She waves again, she gets back on the plane, she waves—no deal ever happens. . . . [29]

BLITZER: You got to close the deal at some point.

TRUMP: Got to make deals. The world is dying to make deals. And we don't have the right people doing it.

BLITZER: The vice president, Dick Cheney.

TRUMP: Well, he's obviously a very hawkish guy on the war. He said the war was going fantastically, just a few months ago. And you know, it's just very sad. I don't know if they're bad people, I don't know what's going on, I just know that they got us into a mess, the likes of which this country has probably never seen. It's one of the great catastrophes of all time. And perhaps even worse, the rest of the world hates us. . . .

BLITZER: How does the United States get out of this situation? Is there a way out?

TRUMP: You know how they get out? They get out. That's how they get out. Declare victory and leave. Because I'll tell you, this country is just going to get further bogged down. They're in a civil war over there, Wolf. There's nothing that we're going to be able to do with a civil war. They are in a major civil war, and it's going to go to Iran, and it's going to go to other countries. . . . Now, President Bush says he's religious, and yet 400,000 people, the way I count it, have died, and probably millions have been badly maimed and injured. What's going on? What's going on? And the day we pull out, it's going to explode. . . .

BLITZER: What do you think of some of these scandals that are unfolding in Washington right now? . . .

TRUMP: Look, everything in Washington has been a lie: weapons of mass destruction—was a total lie. It was a way of attacking Iraq, which he thought was going to be easy and it turned out to be the exact opposite of easy.

It was in its way a scintillating performance, Trump projecting tell-it-like-it-is candor despite being substantively incoherent. No doubt the executives at CNN were pleased. Yet for our purposes, the significance of the exchange is this: As early as 2007, Trump was already market-testing themes that within a decade would make him president.

44 Stanches the Bleeding

On one point at least, Trump was right: The Iraq War had indeed yielded a catastrophe. Bush's Freedom Agenda had stalled in Baghdad. By 2008, with multiple wars ongoing across the Greater Middle East, the world's most powerful nation was strategically in a daze.

Worse still, at the end of 2007, an immense economic upheaval, soon dubbed the Great Recession, nearly brought the United States to its knees. Throughout U.S. history, panics, crashes, and burst bubbles had occurred with distressing regularity. But not since the Great Depression of the 1930s had Americans experienced an economic slump this precipitous and severe. The concept of globalization was taking a drubbing.

With another presidential election approaching, these twin crises—wars gone awry and an economy going down the tubes— riveted the nation. As their hoped-for successor to Bush, Republicans nominated Senator John McCain of Arizona, a Vietnam-era war hero and a plain-spoken, if sometimes intemperate statesman who believed that the ongoing conflict in Iraq was both necessary and winnable. Democrats nominated Senator Barack Obama of Illinois.

His qualifications for high office were ridiculously thin, especially on matters related to national security. Yet Obama was an exemplar of the post–Cold War meritocracy: whip smart, impeccably educated, preternaturally composed, and exuding a palpable sense of "cool." He was also black. In 2008, this turned out to be an unbeatable combination.

In November, Obama defeated McCain handily, his victory, in the estimation of many observers, qualifying as easily the most significant in the nation's entire political history. The expectations raised by Obama's election had less to do with war and recession than with the color of his skin. All presidents upon taking office promise to unify the country. For a sliver of an instant, it seemed as if Obama might actually succeed in doing so, healing the racial divide that had haunted America for centuries.

Soon enough, however, hopes of a black president enabling the nation to overcome racism evaporated. Indeed, expectations of President Obama ushering a post-racial society into existence were absurd from the outset. Here the fiction of presidential near omnipotence, for decades a staple of American politics, found its ultimate expression and definitive refutation. Obama took office at a dire moment in American history. He was expected to save the day. He tried. In the estimation of many Americans, things only got worse.

Once in office, Obama came nowhere close to expunging racism. However inadvertently, he spurred it. To more than a few Americans—call them Trumpers avant la lettre—the Obama presidency was a slap in the face and a threat. The mere presence of a black family living in the White House demonstrated loudly and clearly that things had gone badly awry.

Yet premature Trumpers were not alone in resisting the paradise of a color-blind society. During Obama's presidency, as part of the larger phenomenon of identity politics, differences in skin color became more, not less salient, both politically and culturally. In colleges and universities, in the worlds of art and entertainment, and in journalism, sensitivity to race was especially pronounced. In twenty-first-century America, old-fashioned racism persisted alongside a largely unacknowledged and only slightly less problematic racialism, the one feeding off the other.

So for anyone counting on Obama to inaugurate an era of racial comity, his presidency proved a disappointment, if not a complete bust. Obama partisans will cite reasons to temper that negative assessment, rightly crediting the president with averting the complete collapse of the American economy and ending the Great Recession. They will point to landmark reforms in health care, banking, and consumer protection. Obama signed a major transpacific trade pact and committed the United States to a far-reaching plan for addressing climate change. Negotiators working at his behest also secured an agreement suspending Iranian efforts to develop nuclear weapons and restored diplomatic relations with Cuba. All in all, a commendable list.

Unfortunately, even before Obama managed to publish his memoirs, most of the items on that list had been gutted or annulled. Imagine, if upon becoming president in 1953, Dwight D. Eisenhower had condemned the bombing of Hiroshima as a war crime, abrogated the Truman Doctrine, denounced the Marshall Plan, abandoned NATO, severed diplomatic relations with Israel, and resegregated the armed forces. Harry Truman's ranking among twentieth-century presidents would be considerably lower than it is today. In a sense, this was the misfortune that befell Obama upon his departure from office. His successor immediately set out to dismantle most of what comprised his legacy.

Whether motivated by principle, petulance, or ill-disguised racism, Republican efforts to undo all that Obama had accomplished require us to reinterpret his presidency—even before the initial interpretation has fully formed. If Obamacare, the Paris accord on climate change, the Iran nuclear deal, and restoring U.S. diplomatic ties with Havana don't define his legacy, what does?

Allow me to suggest one possibility: Our forty-fourth president's signature achievement was to briefly prolong the life of the Emerald City consensus. He did this by temporarily propping up elements of that consensus already showing signs of impending failure and pivoting toward a domestic freedom agenda to which his immediate predecessors had given only intermittent attention. In that sense, Obama proved himself a worthy successor to Bill Clinton and George W. Bush. He continued their work and, in doing so, set the stage for the explosive repudiation of November 2016.

Seeking to extend its run, Obama instead rang down the curtain on the post–Cold War era. This likely defines his chief contribution to American history. In that context, the significance of what he accomplished while in office pales in comparison to what happened once he stepped down.

So his achievements, while real, produced ironic results. Three in particular stand out. In each, his efforts inadvertently laid the basis for a powerful backlash.

The first category required Obama to conduct a salvage operation. He saved globalized neoliberalism.

George W. Bush had bequeathed to his successor an economy in free fall, with hundreds of thousands of American jobs being lost each month. Skyrocketing unemployment was headed toward 10 percent of the working population, a figure not seen since 1982. Real estate prices plunged, leaving millions of Americans "under water"—the size of their mortgages exceeding the value of their homes. Mortgage default rates soared. The "Big Three" automobile makers, long a symbol of American industrial might, verged on bankruptcy, as did several storied investment banking firms, among them Lehman Brothers, Merrill Lynch, Goldman Sachs, Bear Stearns, AIG, and the Blackstone Group.

Once in office, Obama and his team, helped by timely action undertaken by the Federal Reserve, pulled the economy out of its nosedive. Key initiatives included a massive $787 billion stimulus bill that Obama signed into law within a month of becoming president, a bailout package for the auto industry, a bit of tax relief for members of the working class, and reduction of the prime interest rate to essentially zero percent.

Overall, this package of initiatives worked—sort of. Housing prices stabilized, unemployment eased, and stock indices began to recover.

Yet this success was hardly without drawbacks. Among them: several years in which the federal deficit exceeded a trillion dollars. During the Bush administration, the national debt had more than doubled to over $11 trillion. During the Obama-engineered recovery, it broke through the $20 trillion barrier.[30] Justified as necessary to restore economic health, these mushrooming deficits suggested that federal authorities had once and for all abandoned even the pretense of minimal fiscal discipline.

Sadly, the mendacity and malfeasance that had paved the way for the Great Recession went essentially unpunished. Through their marketing of complex financial instruments such as mortgage-backed securities and credit default swaps, investment banks had essentially perpetrated a gigantic swindle. Deeming these banks "too big to fail," Obama let off the hook the very predators who had almost destroyed the system from which they handsomely profited. Not for the first time in American history, the malefactors of great wealth got away with their crimes.

Given the havoc it wreaked, the Great Recession might have provided an occasion for critically reassessing the supposed imperatives of globalization. Obama's approach to saving the system ensured that no such reassessment occurred. By the time he prepared to leave office, neoliberal precepts had regained their status as nonnegotiable. The assumption of more growth providing an eventual remedy to income inequality remained intact. And the United States remained what it had been: a nation in which the needs of corporate capitalism take precedence over the common good.

The second element of Obama's legacy relates to the uses of U.S. military power. During the Bush years, militarized global leadership had taken a beating, due largely to the frustrations produced by the Iraq War. Obama's contribution was to modify American militarism and give it a new lease on life, ensuring that the nation's post–Cold War penchant for war would persist.

This was an outcome drenched with irony. After all, no sooner had Obama moved into the White House than the Norwegian Nobel Committee put its stamp of approval on his victory by awarding him its Peace Prize. In a matter of weeks, according to the committee, Obama had "created a new climate in international politics." His "efforts to strengthen international diplomacy and cooperation between peoples" were nothing short of "extraordinary," the committee raved. "Dialogue and negotiations" were once more "preferred as instruments for resolving even the most difficult international conflicts." The prospect of worldwide nuclear disarmament beckoned.[31]

The committee's verdict turned out to be wildly off the mark. As a peacemaker, Obama proved to be a disappointment. Sustaining wars rather than ending them turned out to be his forte. As for nuclear weapons, he ended up initiating a thirty-year, $1.2 trillion program to modernize the American arsenal.[32]

From Bush, Obama had inherited two middle-sized armed conflicts: Iraq and Afghanistan. Each had begun as an integral component of the overarching Global War on Terrorism. By the time Obama became commander in chief, each had acquired a different, if not openly acknowledged, purpose. By 2009, the United States was fighting in Iraq to avoid the humiliation of outright failure. The principal aim was to arrange a graceful exit. Fighting in Afghanistan centered on the right to national self-determination, with Washington intent on allowing Afghans to exercise that right only on the narrowest of terms. The actual aim was to exclude from power in Kabul any group that Washington deemed unacceptable.

Obama's efforts in managing these two wars produced few positive outcomes. In Iraq, he kept to his predecessor's announced schedule for a phased withdrawal, with the last U.S. troops exiting that country in December 2011. Yet that departure proved only temporary. When tested, Iraqi forces, trained and equipped by the United States at great expense, proved unable to defend their country. Less than three years after they had left, U.S. air and ground forces were returning to Iraq, once more engaging in combat operations, this time against an enemy, the Islamic State, created as a by-product of the 2003 invasion. In short order, this revived Iraq War spilled into Syria. U.S. forces followed.

Candidate Obama had vowed to end the Iraq War, characterizing it as "stupid." President Obama failed to make good on that promise, instead bequeathing to his successor a modified version of the war he himself had inherited.

Candidate Obama had vowed to win the Afghanistan War, which he called "necessary." Winning meant eliminating or reducing to insignificance violent opposition to the U.S.-installed government in Kabul. Once in office, President Obama attempted to do just that by ordering a major escalation of the war effort there. He appointed a new commander who promised a fresh approach. He also sent a sizable increment of additional troops into the war zone.

Unfortunately, the ensuing "surge," modeled after the Iraq "surge" of 2007–2008, failed abysmally. The new commander soon departed. Several others followed, each touting his own fresh approach. Over the course of Obama's eight years in office, none came anywhere near to eliminating the militant threat to the Western-installed government in Kabul. As a result, along with ongoing hostilities in Iraq and Syria, the Afghanistan War formed part of Obama's bequest to his successor.

Yet Obama's inability to end these two particular conflicts that he had not started does not capture the real significance of his tenure as commander in chief. It was during his presidency that the very idea of war termination vanished from national security circles. The concept of "forever wars" took hold.

During the 1990s, Bush 41 and then Bill Clinton had chipped away at the reluctance to use force known informally as the Vietnam Syndrome. After 9/11, Bush 43 demolished any surviving remnants of that syndrome, while jettisoning defense and deterrence as the principal rationales for American military power. The Bush Doctrine of preventive war signaled that the United States was going on the offensive. In other words, during the interval between Operation Desert Storm and Operation Iraqi Freedom, these three presidents together engineered the most far-reaching shift in U.S. military policy since the onset of the Korean War in 1950 prompted Harry Truman to order full-scale rearmament.

Obama effectively cemented these changes. As far as war was concerned, the candidate promising "Hope and Change" became a president who delivered a modified version of "More of the Same."

In a democratic society, the key to normalizing war is to divert public attention from its continuing existence. As with air or water pollution, if no one notices, it doesn't matter, at least politically.

Several metrics are available for tabulating the cumulative weight of war. Obvious examples include ordnance expended, targets destroyed, ground gained, dollars spent, enemy killed, or collateral damage inflicted. Yet during the post–Cold War era, only one metric resonated with the broader public: the number of GIs killed in action.

For most of George W. Bush's presidency, the tally of troops killed in action each year hovered slightly below a thousand, a loss rate that contributed to Obama's election in 2008. In the early years of his own presidency, that number dropped to several hundred annually. During his final three years in office, Obama reduced combat losses to a few dozen per year.[33] As that rate trended downward from hundreds to a relative handful, members of the general public, especially those not directly affected by events in far-off combat theaters, began to tune out. In effect, Obama enabled Americans to make their peace with war.

Yet casualty sensitivity did not translate into an aversion to using force. On the contrary, in addition to the ongoing campaign in Afghanistan and the revived campaign in Iraq (spreading into Syria), the 2009 Peace Prize laureate intervened in Libya, renewed operations in Somalia, targeted militant groups in Yemen, established a secret "kill list" to prioritize assassinations, and enlarged the U.S. military "footprint" through much of sub-Saharan Africa. And, of course, he ran Osama bin Laden to ground in Pakistan.

As commander in chief, however, Obama developed his own distinctive approach to waging war. Not quite rising to the level of a doctrine, it served instead as a rough operational proclivity. Especially after his Afghanistan surge failed, he sought to minimize "boots on the ground," relying instead on air power (with a particular preference for missile-firing drones) and small groups of elite special operations forces, usually on missions of limited duration. If large-scale ground combat was required, Obama wanted proxies to do the fighting and dying. So in the final year of his presidency, for example, nearly twenty-five thousand American bombs and missiles rained down on targets in various parts of the planet.[34] Yet total U.S. combat losses that same year numbered twenty-six.[35] Obama's way of war was war conducted at arm's length.

To put it another way, President Obama embraced capabilities touted by proponents of the Revolution in Military Affairs, while modifying their application. In doing so, he abandoned claims that high-tech warfare held the promise of easy and decisive victories. For Obama, results achieved in the field mattered less than the political impact at home. Muting that impact made war tolerable. In effect, the president's own sensitivity to casualties desensitized the public as to what U.S. forces were actually doing, where they were, and what, if anything, they were accomplishing.

The final category of Obama's legacy brings us to the most pronounced difference between Boone City and the Emerald City: the meaning of personal freedom. In Boone City, freedom was allowed to some, but not all. While conferring rights and privileges, freedom also established limits and imposed obligations, a requirement to take up arms in the country's defense in times of emergency not least among them. This was freedom as Al, Fred, and Homer had understood the term.

The promise of the Emerald City was that all should enjoy freedom, not just some. No longer were race, gender, and sexuality to serve as a basis for allocating privilege or for drawing distinctions between what was permitted and what was prohibited. There was also this further difference: In the Emerald City, freedom entailed few duties. As for taking up arms in the country's defense, that had long since become an entirely voluntary proposition.

Bill Clinton had enjoyed limited success in promoting this expanded domestic freedom agenda. George W. Bush had shown little inclination to do so, his attention absorbed by efforts to impose an altogether different Freedom Agenda on Afghans and Iraqis. Under Obama, however, this more capacious conception of American freedom came into its own.

Whether upon entering office Obama saw himself as a culture warrior seems unlikely. Yet during his two terms, the culture war took a seemingly decisive turn, with the patriarchy thrown on the defensive and heteronormativity forfeiting whatever vestiges of moral authority it retained. In progressive circles, at least, celebrating diversity, empowering women, and exploring the variable nature of identity acquired a cachet that combined righteousness with a tinge of smug condescension. That all of this occurred during the tenure of the nation's first black president qualified as either entirely appropriate or absolutely the last straw, depending on one's point of view.

The key event occurred in April 2015 when the Supreme Court heard arguments in the case of *Obergefell v. Hodges*, centering on marriage eligibility. Asking the court to declare unconstitutional state laws prohibiting same-sex marriage, Obama's solicitor general, Donald B. Verrilli, made his case with clarity and directness. "The opportunity to marry is integral to human dignity," he stated. To deny gay and lesbian couples this opportunity was necessarily, therefore, to demean them. Allowing some states to prohibit same-sex marriage while others permitted it was not an option. Doing so would "approximate the house divided we had with de jure racial segregation." As for reasons "once thought necessary and proper" for "ostracizing and marginalizing" gay people, Verrilli found them so without merit that he did not even bother to detail what those reasons had been.[36]

The court concurred with the administration's view. In June 2015, by a narrow 5–4 majority, it issued a ruling requiring all fifty states to recognize same-sex marriage. In his oral argument before the court, Verrilli had suggested that the matter at hand went beyond marriage. The ultimate issue, he observed, was "validation." And so it proved to be, the *Obergefell* decision validating not only same-sex marriage, but also the larger cultural project for which it served as a rallying cry. In effect, while recognizing a hitherto nonexistent right, the court had also nullified norms "once thought necessary and proper" to ordering social relationships.

In terms of significance, *Obergefell* compares with *Brown v. Board of Education* or *Roe v. Wade*. The *New York Times*, the nation's most influential institutional advocate of gay rights, hailed it as "a profound and inspiring opinion expanding human rights across America, and bridging the nation's past to its present." In a sense, it was that. In another sense, however, rather than erecting a bridge, the decision acknowledged an immense fissure. Indeed, as the *Times* itself noted with barely concealed glee, *Obergefell* left opponents of same-sex marriage struggling "to fathom how the country they thought they understood could so rapidly pass them by."[37]

Substitute *defined* or *embodied* for *understood* and the judgment fits. Indeed, as recently as 2008, Obama himself had numbered among those who opposed gay marriage.[38] By 2015, however, the president had revised his views, welcoming *Obergefell* as a decision that affirmed "what millions of Americans already believe in their hearts: When all Americans are treated as equal, we are all more free."[39]

Such sentiments struck me then, and still do today, as too glib by half. While equality may enhance the possibility of freedom, it by no means guarantees the intelligent use of freedom. Obama's judgment cast the issue in quantitative terms when the problems facing twenty-first-century Americans are primarily qualitative. What Americans need is not more freedom but truer freedom, grounded in something other than the reiteration of comforting clichés.

I admire President Obama greatly and voted for him twice. Once, during his second term, he invited me to lunch with him in the White House. It was, for me at least, a memorable occasion. I came away from the encounter deeply impressed by his intelligence, grace, wit, mastery of detail, and sense of self-possession.

Yet I view his eight years in office with a mixture of sadness and dismay. More than anything else, his presidency represented a missed opportunity.

While nursing the economy back toward some semblance of health, Obama left untouched the egregious disparities of wealth that globalized neoliberalism fosters and that make a mockery of democracy. In twenty-first-century America, substantive freedom has increasingly become the privilege of the moneyed class.

Obama avoided large-scale military catastrophes, for which I was grateful. Yet he did little to curb American militarism. Global leadership remained largely synonymous with the use of force. The war machine churned on, with most citizens all but numb to its existence. In the year of Obama's birth, President Dwight D. Eisenhower had decried the rise of what he called the military-industrial complex. In doing so, Ike performed a last great service for his countrymen. Yet a phrase coined in 1961 does not adequately describe the militarized mindset to which Washington had succumbed since the end of the Cold War. In contrast to Ike, Obama did next to nothing to educate Americans about the dangers this mindset poses.

As for the revised conception of freedom, I may not possess the qualifications to offer an opinion. An aging white heterosexual male approaching a half century of monogamous marriage and with one foot still stuck in Boone City should be careful about instructing fellow citizens who are younger, not white, not hetero, and/or not male on how they should assess the cultural upheaval that reached a climax of sorts while Obama was president. Possessing neither a smartphone nor a social media account, I lack the most basic tools for doing so. Even so, I would caution against concluding that liberating the individual from traditional bonds of self-restraint has brought the Promised Land into view. Spiritual torpor strikes me as a more probable outcome.

On that point, as a self-declared admirer of Reinhold Niebuhr, Obama might have alerted Americans to the dangers of nursing "Messianic dreams" regarding history's purpose and destination. Breaking free of the nation's racist, sexist, and homophobic past suggested the possibility that Americans, singing "their odes to liberty," might finally fulfill their vocation to align humanity with their own quest for perfect freedom—in many respects the central conceit of the entire post–Cold War era. Of the three post–Cold War presidents, only Obama knew better than to indulge that conceit. Only Obama understood that, as Niebuhr had written, "the course of history cannot be coerced . . . in accordance with a particular conception of its end." He should have said so bluntly and repeatedly.[40]

Donald Trump did not share my admiration for President Obama. During the Obama era, he busied himself hosting *The Apprentice* (alternately *Celebrity Apprentice*), a "reality" TV series that showcased his ostensible talents as an astute, no-nonsense business executive. The show's success, inexplicable to critics, boosted him higher in the ranks of B-list celebrities, even if in the huckster vein. By peddling a twenty-first-century version of "the stuff that dreams are made of," Trump was also beating his own drum, courtesy of NBC and the show's corporate sponsors.

Meanwhile, his central political preoccupation was to question Obama's eligibility to serve as president. While Donald Trump did not invent "birtherism," he embraced the cause wholeheartedly and became its highest-profile proponent. His approach was not to present facts but to raise doubts about Obama's birthplace, religion, and upbringing and therefore to keep alive questions about whether this black man with an unusual name should have been allowed to run for president in the first place. With the media generously providing a platform, Trump praised birthers as "great people" and expounded at length on his suspicions that there was "something fishy" going on.[41] Hard facts were few in number, but as always Trump was good for ratings.

Obama used the occasion of the 2011 White House Correspondents' Dinner, with Trump in attendance, to respond. His official birth certificate having just been made public, the president speculated that no one was happier than Trump to have the controversy put to rest. The tycoon-turned-TV host, Obama continued, could now focus on "the issues that matter," such as "Did we fake the moon landing?" and "Where are Biggie and Tupac?" Just hours before, the president had greenlighted the super-secret Operation Neptune Spear that within days would result in the death of Osama bin Laden. Now he proceeded to mock Trump's "credentials and breadth of experience," citing a recent episode of *Celebrity Apprentice* that had required him to fix responsibility for a botched cooking competition—"the kind of decision," Obama cracked, "that would keep me up at night. Well handled, sir!"[42]

Obama's skewering of Trump qualified as both well deserved and decidedly vicious. Those in attendance laughed uproariously at Trump's expense. Yet the last laugh would be his.

6

STATE OF THE UNION

What sort of place was America in 2016 as the post–Cold War era reached the quarter-century mark? With the nation bracing itself for another presidential election, the prospect of a contest pitting another Clinton against another Bush beckoned. "Newsflash: It's Going to Be Hillary vs. Jeb"—so concluded *Politico* even before ballots had been cast in the nation's first primary.[1]

Some found this anticipated clash of rival dynasties reassuring. For others, it offered evidence of a disturbingly inbred and self-perpetuating political elite. Few observers, however, anticipated the thunderclap that would sound before year's end. Yet with the benefit of hindsight, we can identify plentiful evidence that presaged its coming.

Encompassing 3.8 million square miles, divided into nearly ninety thousand distinct political jurisdictions, and with a population approaching 325 million, the United States of America is a mammoth enterprise—perhaps too big for its own good.[2] Politicians seeking high office invariably agree that on balance their country is the best ever, albeit one that will become more wonderful still should they be elected. This quadrennial song and dance suffices to placate (or anesthetize) the broad political center, a.k.a. the Great American Middle Class, thereby confining national politics to a predictably narrow channel. Would-be presidents who stray from that channel invariably meet with rejection.

The election of 2016 would prove to be different. What follows is a snapshot or profile of America as that election approached, highlighting factors that coalesced by November to install Donald Trump as president. With stunning suddenness, the center gave way, exposing a country already divided into two starkly antagonistic camps. Yet for anyone not beguiled by visions of the Emerald City, signs of that division were everywhere.

Bud Light vs. Small-Batch Bourbon

The United States is the world's greatest democracy. For Americans, that statement qualifies as an unimpeachable fact. Yet during the post–Cold War era, privilege and inequality emerged as dominant traits of that democracy. In a nation that had once prided itself on being immune to class distinctions—simply being an American sufficed as an identity—such distinctions were becoming omnipresent, everywhere from the seating at professional sports venues to the boarding sequence in air travel. As never before in history, F. Scott Fitzgerald's pithy observation about the rich "being different from you and me" expressed an essential truth about American life.[3]

In 2016, according to *Forbes* magazine, there were 540 billionaires in the United States, with a combined net worth of $2.399 trillion.[4] On the *Forbes* list of the four hundred wealthiest Americans, Donald Trump's fortune, then estimated at $3.7 billion, was only good enough for a ranking of 156.[5] Wealth is relative. In comparison with Bill Gates ($81 billion) or Jeff Bezos ($67 billion), he qualified as only moderately well to do. Even so, he fell comfortably within the top 1 percent of earners, a group controlling more than one-third of the nation's entire wealth. In contrast, the bottom 50 percent of the population made do with a mere 1 percent of it.

Since the earliest days of the republic, the United States had offered material abundance for some while condemning others to lives of want or outright squalor. America was a land of opportunity, but not for all. By 2016, even as globalization was touted as working to the benefit of everyone, the gap between haves and have-nots had grown to somewhere between cavernous and grotesque. By way of illustration, compare the average earnings of CEOs with those of employees. In 1965, this so-called compensation ratio had been 20:1; in 1989, 59:1; by 2016, it had mushroomed to 271:1.[6]

Yet in national politics, such disparities possessed minimal resonance. Although the plight of the poor—at least forty-three million Americans were living in poverty that year—qualified as a matter of regret, it generated only local and episodic political interest.[7] According to polling data, poverty and income disparity ranked at the very bottom of problems that mattered to Americans.[8] Politically speaking, both had seemingly become tolerable.

By election year 2016, moreover, the Great Recession was fast fading into memory. After shedding nearly nine million jobs between 2007 and 2010, the economy had begun turning around. The employment picture steadily improved.[9] By the summer of 2016, as the Republican and Democratic parties were settling on their presidential nominees, the unemployment rate had fallen to 4.7 percent, less than half what it had been in 2010.[10] Stock prices were soaring.[11]

Amid such signs of recovery, the nation's political establishment continued its spendthrift ways. Although the annual federal budget deficit had fallen from its trillion-dollar-per-annum peak during the Great Recession, in 2016 the government still spent $587 billion more than it took in.[12] Just servicing the national debt now cost the government nearly $300 billion yearly—more than the combined budgets of the Agriculture, Commerce, Education, Energy, Homeland Security, Housing and Urban Development, State, and Treasury Departments.[13] As usual, Republicans went through the motions of calling for a balanced budget, once seen as a minimal standard of good governance. As a practical matter, they were no more interested in balancing the budget than they were in amending the Constitution to allow prayer in public schools. Both numbered among the promises commonly made by GOP candidates while campaigning, only to be forgotten once they gained power.

Although the economy was recovering, the benefits were anything but evenly distributed. For most Americans the aftermath of bust was something other than boom. The rich were once again getting richer, but the take-home pay of working-class Americans remained stagnant, as it had for decades.[14] And the shuttering of factories that had long sustained the middle class—4.5 million manufacturing jobs lost since the passage of NAFTA in 1994—continued.[15] Globalization was accelerating the deindustrialization of the U.S. economy, exporting more jobs than it was creating. As for those Americans born into poverty, they were likely to die poor as well: Studies revealed a sharp decline in social mobility dating back to the 1980s, but worsening in the wake of the Cold War.[16]

Globalization was supposed to lift all boats. Instead, it was leaving millions stranded. By 2016, evidence of acute economic distress and insecurity was evident, even among those fortunate enough to have jobs. For example, credit card debt that year exceeded a trillion dollars, averaging $8,377 per household.[17] Similarly, with pensions becoming a thing of the past, the median retirement savings for all

American families in 2016 came to a measly $5,000.[18] Black and Hispanic families fared even worse, with most having no retirement savings at all.[19] In effect, most retirees faced the prospect of subsisting entirely on social security. Yet the average monthly social security check that year amounted to only $1,404.[20]

Other indicators of economic hardship included a homeless population averaging 549,000 on any given night; 44.2 million Americans who were receiving food assistance from the federal Supplemental Nutrition Assistance Program (SNAP); and 30 million schoolchildren receiving low-cost or free school lunches.[21]

All these statistics were readily available. Some occasionally made the news. Yet they all fell into the category of what former defense secretary Donald Rumsfeld notoriously called "known knowns." To be more precise, they numbered among the matters more or less accepted as mere background noise.

Such data points do not, of course, provide a balanced or comprehensive picture of the American economy or of American well-being in 2016. For those with disposable income at hand, everyday life in the United States could be very good indeed—far superior to what it had been back when Al, Fred, and Homer returned from their war. The cuisine was more varied, the coffee better tasting, the offerings of wine, cheese, and other comestibles at local grocers more interesting—all this coming at a price, of course.

Opportunities for diversion, whether participatory or vicarious, were becoming almost literally infinite. Americans flocked to theme parks such as Orlando, Florida's Disney World and Universal Studios, which were becoming bigger, better, and more expensive, the per person price of a one-day pass now reaching $115.[22] The expansion of Major League Baseball to thirty teams, the NFL to thirty-two, the NBA to thirty, and the NHL to thirty-one brought almost every American into the penumbra of some big-league city and with it opportunities to spend money rooting for the home team.

For those who could afford it, information technology offered convenience, choice, entertainment, and a simulacrum of community. With the right device and the right subscription, Americans could enjoy instant access to just about every song ever recorded, every television series ever broadcast, and every surviving movie going back to the silent era. With a click of a mouse, almost any product known to humankind, from Chinese takeout to embroidered silk pajamas, could be delivered to your doorstep, depending on your zip code, in as little as an hour.

Foreign travel, once considered exotic except for U.S. military personnel, had become routine. In 2016, just shy of 67 million Americans went abroad, while 11.5 million piled aboard cruise liners to vacation afloat.[23] That same year, Americans lost $116.9 billion gambling and spent another $70 billion on lottery tickets.[24] For those who had already made their killing, there were private jets, opulent yachts, and second (or third) homes overlooking the water or situated alongside mountains.

So life could be very good indeed for those in a position to enjoy it. Yet these indicators of an enhanced quality of life and of a collective determination to have a good time had minimal relevance to the political climate existing in 2016. What actually mattered was this: On a daily basis, tens of millions of Americans were enduring what one writer that year called "financial impotence."[25] These were not the poorest of the poor, but those persuaded that the deck was stacked against them.

These Americans were not shopping at gourmet delis, wearing overpriced sneakers, or ponying up $849 per ticket to see *Hamilton* on Broadway.[26] To put food on the table and pay the rent, they were living from paycheck to paycheck, with virtually nothing to spare for unexpected emergencies. If they were buying scratch tickets, it was out of some desperate hope that Lady Luck might deliver them from straitened circumstances. Rather than beneficiaries of globalized neoliberalism, they saw themselves as its dupes.

In the 2016 election, financial impotence was to turn into political outrage, bringing the post–Cold War era to an abrupt end. As for the people who shop for produce at Whole Foods, wear vintage jeans, and ski in Aspen, they never saw it coming and couldn't believe it when it occurred.

Call of Duty

In post–Cold War America, one of the most revealing, if largely overlooked, expressions of class is the inverse relationship between wealth and likelihood of being killed or wounded in service to the country. Here, too, was another known known, which prior to the presidential election of 2016 many Americans had come to accept as a given.

In post–Cold War America, the rich, famous, and powerful had an aversion to active military service, matched only by their professed regard for those who did serve. At least nominally, to be a veteran had once more become a mark of distinction. Yet it was a mark that members of the elite could easily do without.

Prince Harry, grandson of the Queen of England, served two tours of duty in Afghanistan, the second as a crewmember on an AH-64 Apache attack helicopter. No one today expects the children or grandchildren of an American head of state, corporate bigwig, or Hollywood celebrity to do likewise.

Even though the United States has been continuously at war since 2001, the Venn diagram of the young, fit, and privileged and of those killed or wounded in action consists of twin circles that barely touch. Pat Tillman, the NFL player who enlisted in the army after 9/11, deployed to Afghanistan in 2004, and lost his life there in a friendly fire incident, remains a singularly anomalous figure in recent American history. No other professional athlete or comparably significant personage has followed his patriotic example.

In that regard, Donald Trump and his offspring qualify as exemplary upper-class Americans. During the Vietnam War, Trump avoided military service, this at a time when dodging the draft qualified as somewhere between righteous and commonsensical. His children and their spouses have followed in the family tradition. With military service officially optional, they have seen fit to opt out, as have most other well-to-do Americans.

So in the nation's recent wars, who actually does the fighting and dying? Do the casualties incurred represent a cross section of the American people in all of their wondrous variety? Simply put, no.

In post–Cold War America, diversity rivals inclusiveness as the dominant cultural leitmotif. More diverse necessarily signifies better. Or put another way, evidence of inequality and shortfalls in diversity, especially pertaining to race, gender, and sexual orientation, are by definition problems that demand concerted remedial action.

To this otherwise binding dictum, there exists one glaring exception: military service. In a nation that is now permanently at war, elite institutions that otherwise pride themselves on their commitment to diversity don't go out of their way to recruit veterans, to put it mildly. So in 2016, for example, the undergraduate student body at Princeton included exactly one veteran. Harvard College and Williams each had three vets, Duke none, Yale a whopping eleven.[27] These figures have yet to evoke an outcry of protest from university faculties keen to ensure the equitable representation of women and people of color and acutely sensitive to the slightest evidence of discrimination based on sexuality.

As for diversity within the military itself, highly publicized instances of tokenism—female officers becoming fighter pilots or graduating from the army's Ranger School—divert attention from gaping inequities related to class. When it comes to socioeconomic status, the armed forces come nowhere close to looking like America.

Noteworthy on this point is the fact that the Pentagon, with its otherwise nearly insatiable appetite for data, does not collect (or at least release) information regarding the socioeconomic status of American casualties. Observance of this unofficial taboo conceals who is doing the bleeding and dying on the nation's behalf.

As scholars Douglas Kriner and Francis Shen have shown, when it comes to military sacrifice in the post–Cold War era, there exist "Two Americas." Kriner and Shen provide a wealth of empirical evidence showing that wealthier communities suffer far fewer casualties than do less affluent ones. "Even more than previous wars," they wrote, "Iraq and Afghanistan have been working class wars," with the poorer parts of America "bearing a greater share of the human costs of war."[28] It's not residents of Palo Alto, California, or Manhattan's Upper East Side who suffer the greatest incidence of combat-related post-traumatic stress or traumatic brain injury or multiple amputations.

Kriner and Shen substantiate what nonacademic observers have long suspected. In no sense do the armed forces of the United States represent a cross section of American society. In March 2003, with the Iraq War barely under way, for example, the *New York Times* matter-of-factly likened the composition of the armed forces to the "makeup of a two-year commuter or trade school outside Birmingham or Biloxi."[29] Had the *Times* characterized the school's student body as largely male, it would have aptly characterized the cohort that has done most of the fighting in recent American wars.

In post–Cold War America, college is all about good times and the prospect of upward mobility. In contrast, serving in the armed forces of the United States, especially in the army or Marine Corps, offers the nontrivial possibility of being killed or maimed. So apart from rare exceptions like the late Corporal Tillman, inducing prospective soldiers to sign up entails appealing to something more compelling than love of country. It requires that most American of motivators: money.

Here we come face-to-face with the dirty little secret of the contemporary American military system: The so-called all-volunteer force (AVF) is something other than what its name implies. Absent sufficiently generous material incentives, the AVF would fold up faster than Trump Airlines, the Trump Taj Mahal, and Trump University.

In post–Cold War America, opportunities for those lacking a college diploma are limited. The Pentagon is one of a dwindling number of employers offering youngsters fresh out of high school jobs that come with decent pay, comprehensive medical benefits, and the prospect of a guaranteed pension, if they live long enough to claim it. Globalization might be depleting the domestic manufacturing sector, but in doing so it replenishes the supply of potential enlistees—all those high school grads looking for something better to do than busing tables or working the checkout counter at Walmart.

So for Americans of means, military service may represent a genuinely free choice. For everyone else, inducements in the form of salary, bonuses, benefits, and special incentive pay influence that choice, in many instances decisively.

The expenditures required to sustain the ranks of the AVF are formidable. The U.S. Army alone spends $300 million annually in advertising and enlistment bonuses, with new recruits offered as much as $40,000 just for signing up.[30] Additional bonuses entice soldiers to reenlist.

So the all-volunteer force is not so much recruited as bought and paid for. Once post–Cold War soldiers have signed on the dotted

line, of course, they become what their forebears since the founding of the Republic have been: instruments of the state. As such,
they become subject to involuntary participation in any and all military undertakings that the state may devise, with no informed
consent required.

What distinguishes today's soldiers from earlier generations,
whether conscripts or volunteers, is their relationship not to the state
but to their fellow citizens. Prior to the post–Cold War era, three
large themes had governed the relationship between citizens and
soldiers. During extended periods of peace—the 1920s and 1930s,
for instance—most Americans paid little attention to those who
served. During conflicts deemed justifiable and necessary—World
War II and the early Cold War, for example—Americans warmly
supported the troops, with elite participation in military service
one concrete manifestation of that support. Wars deemed unjusti-
fied and unnecessary—Vietnam providing the best example—found
substantial numbers of Americans, representatives of the elite very
much in the vanguard, mobilizing in opposition and undermining
the very legitimacy of the existing military system.

The post–Cold War era recast the relationship between the
American people and their military. Today, Americans have become
inured to war and to an accompanying atmosphere of never-ending
national security emergency. Although participating in rituals
intended to convey support for the troops, they remain steadfastly
indifferent to what the troops are actually doing. Questions about
whether our working-class wars are justifiable, necessary, or even
winnable go largely unasked. Meanwhile, as those conflicts drag on
or meander toward some ill-defined conclusion, elites neither par-
ticipate nor protest, but devote themselves to matters they find
more agreeable or urgent. The troops themselves are left holding
the bag.

Is this arrangement democratic? Fair? Morally defensible? If nothing else, does it at least produce beneficial outcomes? Honesty demands a negative response to each of those questions. As the post–Cold War era unfolded, however, honesty in establishment circles proved to be in short supply. Reciting empty banalities—thank you for your service!—was thought to suffice. Yet as the 2016 election approached, any office seeker willing to question the sense of U.S. military policies stood a good chance of getting a hearing from working-class citizens directly exposed to the consequences of an ill-advised infatuation with war.

The end of the Cold War had ostensibly conferred on the United States military capabilities beyond compare, which authorities in Washington were raring to put to use. But as with globalization, so, too, with a militarized approach to global leadership: The victims of an experiment concocted by elites would prove to have only a limited willingness to absorb punishment. Indeed, after a quarter of a century, their patience was all but exhausted.

No Rules, Just Rights

"At the heart of liberty is the right to define one's own concept of existence, of meaning, of the universe, and of the mystery of human life."[31] So wrote Supreme Court Justice Anthony Kennedy in a famous decision handed down shortly after the Cold War ended.

Kennedy's reformulation of liberty, however grandiose, was well suited to the mood that swept through elite quarters at the end of history. By comparison, the inalienable rights specified in the famous Declaration of 1776 now seemed cramped, stingy, and inadequate. With the Emerald City visible on the horizon, freedom itself was in line for a makeover.

The emerging post–Cold War conception of freedom was nothing if not expansive. It recognized few limits and imposed fewer obligations, with one notable exception: Compliance was nonnegotiable. As always, the American definition of liberty, however recently revised, was universally applicable, as valid in Bogotá and Dakar as in Boston and Denver.

What did this signify in practice? Allowing individuals maximum latitude to reach their own conclusions regarding the concepts of existence, meaning, the universe, and the mystery of human life yielded what sort of society? The quarter century that elapsed between the fall of the Berlin Wall and Donald Trump's election as U.S. president provided a tentative answer to that question.

Part of that answer came in the form of progress toward eliminating the remaining vestiges of racism, empowering women, and reducing discrimination experienced by LGBTQI Americans. Granted, progress does not imply decisive and irreversible success. Yet during the post–Cold War period, American society became more tolerant, more open, more accepting, and less judgmental. Attitudes toward people of color, women, and gays that in the 1950s had been normative and remained widespread in the 1960s and 1970s had by 2016 become unacceptable in polite society.

Yet for more than a few Americans, Justice Kennedy's notion of liberty as an opportunity to ponder life's ultimate questions had little relevance. In practical terms, the exercise of freedom, undertaken in an environment in which consumption and celebrity had emerged as preeminent values, encouraged conformity rather than independence. At least notionally, Americans now enjoyed more freedom than ever before. Yet from every direction, but especially from Madison Avenue, Hollywood, and Silicon Valley, came cues for how to make the most of the freedom now on offer. And however much you had, you always needed more.

So along with freedom came stress, anxiety, and a sense of not quite measuring up or a fear of falling behind as the demands of daily life seemed to multiply. For some, freedom meant alien-ation, anomie, and despair. It did nothing to prevent, and in some instances arguably fostered, self-destructive or antisocial behavior.

So in 2016, as another presidential election approached, Ameri-cans were able to claim the following distinctions:

- One in six were taking prescription psychiatric drugs such as anti-depressants or antianxiety medication.[32]
- Over sixteen million adults and over three million adolescents were suffering from significant depression.[33]
- More than 1.9 million Americans were regularly using cocaine, with a half million hooked on heroin and 700,000 on metham-phetamines.[34]
- That year opioid overdoses killed forty-six thousand, a new rec-ord.[35]
- Binge drinking had reached epidemic proportions, with one in six U.S. adults binge drinking several times a month and consum-ing seven drinks per binge; according to the Centers for Disease Control and Prevention, binging was especially common among younger and more affluent Americans.[36]
- Nearly forty-five thousand were taking their own lives annually, the national suicide rate having increased by 24 percent since 1999; within the previous decade the suicide rate of teenage girls had doubled and of boys had jumped by 40 percent.[37]
- Cellphone addiction was joining more traditional compulsions, with the average person checking his or her cellphone 110 times a day, impelled by FOMO—a fear of missing out (often on the absurdly trivial).[38]
- Compulsive buying syndrome, a.k.a. shopping addiction, afflicted an estimated 6 percent of the population; a comparable number were compulsive hoarders.[39]

- On a daily basis eleven million Americans, mostly women, struggled with eating disorders such as anorexia and bulimia.[40]

- Roughly 40 percent of adults and nearly 19 percent of children and adolescents were obese.[41]

- Cosmetic surgeons were performing over seventeen million procedures annually, with buttock augmentation and labiaplasty enjoying a particular spike in popularity.[42]

- Forty million Americans were regularly visiting online porn sites.[43]

- The number of Americans infected with sexually transmitted diseases in 2016 surpassed two million, according to the CDC, "the highest number ever."[44]

- Between 40 percent and 50 percent of all marriages, most presumably undertaken with expectations of permanence, were ending in divorce.[45]

- An estimated 24.7 million children were growing up in fatherless households, with such children substantially more likely to drop out of school, abuse drugs and alcohol, and commit suicide; girls raised without a father present were four times more likely to get pregnant as teenagers.[46]

- Although difficult to quantify with precision, an estimated 683,000 American children in 2016 were victims of abuse or neglect.[47]

- Exercising their right to choose, American women were terminating over 650,000 unwanted pregnancies each year, despite the widespread availability of contraceptives.[48]

- Exercising their right to bear arms, Americans had accumulated 46 percent of the planet's small arms; the U.S. arsenal in private hands was larger than that of the next twenty-five countries combined.[49]

- Meanwhile, more than thirty-three thousand Americans were being killed in firearms-related incidents annually.[50]

- Year in and year out, the United States had the world's highest incarceration rate, no other developed nation coming anywhere close.[51]

- Polling data showed that social trust—how Americans felt about government institutions and their fellow citizens—had sunk to an all-time low.[52]

- Perhaps for that reason, when it came to voting, most Americans couldn't be bothered; voter turnout in the United States lagged behind that of most other developed countries.[53]

- In an increasingly networked society, with two-thirds of Americans on Facebook, chronic loneliness afflicted a large portion of the population.[54]

- In a phenomenon described as "deaths by despair," the life expectancy of white working-class American males was dropping, a trend without historical precedent.[55]

- For the first time in U.S. history, the nation's birthrate had fallen below the rate needed to sustain a stable overall population; America had ceased to reproduce itself.[56]

Not to be overlooked, in their pursuit of life, liberty, and happiness, Americans were polluting, wasting food, and generating trash with abandon, leading the world in each category.[57]

Yet as a particularly noteworthy emblem of post–Cold War freedom, I would nominate tattoos, a.k.a. "body art, body bling, self-graffiti, walking billboards, [and] fashionable ink accessories."[58] By 2016, this had become all the rage, with something like 40 percent of Americans born after 1980 sporting at least one tattoo and/or piercing somewhere other than an earlobe. For the more adventuresome, there was scarification (etching or cutting to produce a design on the skin) or subdermal implants (objects inserted under the skin for ornamental purposes).[59] Here was an especially colorful expression of the obsessively narcissistic turn in the American understanding of liberty that followed the end of history.

A Society Under Duress

Arguably, Americans were enjoying more freedom than ever. Were they happier as a consequence? Polls suggested otherwise. In the 2007 "world happiness" standings, the United States had ranked third among developed countries. By 2016, its position had plummeted to fourteenth.[60]

By no means am I suggesting that a single such statistic holds the key to assessing life in contemporary America. It does not. Nor do the various penchants and pathologies enumerated above. Yet taken together, they suggest a society in which discontent, dysfunction, and sheer perversity were rampant.

As with globalized neoliberalism, some Americans not only coped with seemingly limitless freedom, but also luxuriated in the opportunities that it offered. For sophisticates inhabiting Brooklyn's Park Slope, radical autonomy could well prove to be a boon; for those stuck in a ghetto on Chicago's South Side, not so much. As for the accompanying underside, those in possession of sufficient resources could insulate themselves from its worst effects—just as the affluent were able to insulate themselves from the accumulating post–Cold War military misadventures by simply allowing others to shoulder the burden.

As for the final element of the post–Cold War consensus—expecting presidents to demonstrate the attributes of oracle, moral arbiter, and supreme warlord—as the election of 2016 approached, it remained solidly intact. Bill Clinton, George W. Bush, and Barack Obama may each have come up short, but expectations of the next president delivering the nation to the Emerald City persisted.

What role did Donald Trump play in shaping this America that worked nicely for some while leaving many others adrift and vulnerable? None at all. Globalization, the pursuit of militarized hegemony, a conception of freedom conferring rights without duties, and a political system centered on a quasi-monarchical chief of state each turned out to have a substantial downside. Yet the defects of each made their appearance well before Trump's entry into politics, even if elites, held in thrall by the post–Cold War outlook, were slow to appreciate their significance. None of those defects can be laid at his feet.

If anything, Trump himself had displayed a considerable aptitude for turning such defects to his own advantage. In post–Cold War America, he was prominent among those who enriched themselves, lived large, and let others do the dirty work, while also shielding themselves from the difficulties that made life a trial for many of their fellow citizens. In an era of con artists, cowards, and cynics, Trump became a modern equivalent of P. T. Barnum, parlaying the opportunities at hand into fortune, celebrity, lots of golf, plenty of sex, and eventually the highest office in the land.

Yet for our purposes, the key point is this: Trump did not create the conditions in which the campaign of 2016 was to take place. Instead, to a far greater extent than any of his political rivals, he demonstrated a knack for translating those conditions into votes. Here the moment met the man.

7

PLEBISCITE

Nothing quite like the presidential election of 2016 had ever occurred in the long and colorful history of American politics. Of the nearly two dozen candidates who threw their hat in the ring, the least qualified came out on top. The eventual winner combined Theodore Roosevelt's brashness, Woodrow Wilson's self-regard, Franklin Roosevelt's faux religiosity, John F. Kennedy's serial infidelities, and Lyndon Johnson's crude vulgarity. When speaking, Donald Trump was the inverse of the diffident and self-effacing Calvin Coolidge. Silent Cal's default mode was reticence. Trump didn't know when to shut up. In his disregard for truth, he more than matched Richard Nixon. And in his ability to rally the angry and dispossessed while posing as their champion, he was the Second Coming of Huey Long, the Depression-era populist from Louisiana. Not since the Kingfish himself, his presidential ambitions ended by an assassin's bullet in 1935, had a demagogue of comparable skill appeared on the national political scene.

From the day he famously rode down that escalator at Trump Tower to announce his candidacy, antipathy toward Trump pervaded the upper echelons of the nation's journalistic, political, intellectual, and artistic establishments. In terms of style and personality, he embodied everything that its members professed to loathe. That his own personal qualities—vanity, self-regard, and sleaziness— expressed in grotesquely exaggerated form inclinations pervading the contemporary scene only accentuated that loathing. Trump's political ascent made it far more difficult to sustain the pretense that the consensus forged after the Cold War had given rise to a society worthy of admiration and emulation.

Those benefiting from that consensus were not prepared to consider that it might be deeply and irreparably flawed. That it might soon be discarded in favor of an altogether different set of propositions was simply inconceivable.

So those most deeply invested in globalized neoliberalism or militarized hegemony or radical individual autonomy (or some combination of the three), while counting on the occupant of the White House to serve their cause, greeted Trump's sudden arrival at center stage in American life as equivalent to the abrupt appearance of some dread disease. Restoring the body politic to good health required immediate corrective action. Few of those eager to grasp the scalpel were prepared to consider the possibility that Trump himself might be not the disease, but merely a particularly repulsive symptom of an already well-established, if still undiagnosed, affliction. Virtually none were willing to grant the possibility that Trump filled a legitimate need, that his historical function, whether assigned by Fate, Providence, or a God with a wicked sense of humor, was to make it impossible to ignore any longer the anomalies and incongruities to which the post–Cold War period had given rise.

What led so many Americans to prefer Donald Trump to his Republican rivals and so many others either to withhold their vote from Hillary Clinton or to conclude that voting itself was not worth the time or trouble? Let me posit that the actions of those who supported Trump and those who simply stayed home—together totaling approximately 171 million adult citizens—represented an entirely understandable, if regrettable, response to the trajectory of events that had occurred since the end of the Cold War.

Al, Fred, and Homer would never have taken Trump seriously as a would-be president. By 2016, however, his bombast and talent for self-promotion captured and expressed the underside of the prevailing culture. His candidacy was simultaneously preposterous and more than slightly nauseating. It was also somehow fitting.

Indeed, by the twenty-first century, the values that Trump embodied had become as thoroughly and authentically American as any of those specified in the oracular pronouncements of Thomas Jefferson or Abraham Lincoln or Franklin Roosevelt.

Trump's critics saw him as an abomination. Perhaps he was. Yet he was also very much a man of his time.

Bernie Ignites

But we begin with the candidate who was in some respects Trump's polar opposite and in others his doppelgänger. Like Trump, Senator Bernie Sanders was born in New York City in the 1940s. Biographical similarities pretty much end there. Sanders, after all, became a Vermonter, a self-professed socialist, and a career politician.

In his contribution to the politics of 2016, Sanders reprised the role that former vice president and inveterate New Dealer Henry Wallace had played back in the election of 1948. As a candidate for president, each was a dark horse; yet simply by speaking his mind and refusing to go away, each became an annoying burr under the saddle of the political establishment.

While careful to observe bourgeois conventions, Wallace and Sanders were revolutionaries, intent on reorienting American politics in a fundamentally different direction. Each rejected existing assumptions about what was necessary or possible. Each harped on issues that party leaders preferred to discount or ignore. For Wallace, the issue was a fear of Communism that he deemed inordinate and that was diverting the attention of the Democratic Party from more pressing concerns such as poverty and racism. For Sanders, the issue was the growth of extreme economic inequality, attributable in his view to the excesses of corporate capitalism—tolerated, if not actively abetted, by political elites, including Democrats who were in the pocket of Wall Street and the plutocrats.

Wallace's critique of obsessive anti-Communism proved ill-timed. His challenge to the status quo quickly fizzled out. In contrast, the critique of corporate capitalism fashioned by Sanders in 2016 resonated with a considerable segment of the disenchanted. Rather than fizzling out, it proved to be improbably durable.

Since 2007, Sanders had represented his state in the Senate, caucusing with the Democrats. Yet only occasionally did he admit to formal membership in the Democratic Party, preferring instead to identify himself as an independent. For Sanders, independence meant staking out positions on what qualified in American politics as the Far Left. In 2016, only a single member of the Senate "outscored" him as a bona fide left-winger.[1]

By no stretch of the imagination did Sanders qualify as a leader of the Senate, in either a moral or a practical sense. Prior to his decision to run for president, he had amassed a negligible record of legislative achievement.[2] Beyond the confines of New England, he enjoyed limited name recognition. He had little money, just about no campaign organization, and almost none of the practiced smarminess of the typical pol. When speaking, he came across as impatient and prickly.

The media, therefore, greeted his candidacy as somewhere between quixotic and something of a lark. In prefacing its report on his intention to run, the *Washington Post* described Sanders as "an ex-hippie, septuagenarian socialist from the liberal reaches of Vermont who rails, in his thick Brooklyn accent, rumpled suit and frizzy pile of white hair, against the 'billionaire class' taking over the country."[3] In case you missed the point, as far as the *Post* was concerned, Sanders did not qualify as presidential timber.

Keep in mind that, even before Hillary Clinton had formally announced her candidacy, the nation's sharpest political minds had already anointed the former First Lady, senator, and secretary of state as the Democratic nominee for president in 2016. After all, Clinton had credentials, name recognition, organization, and money. Moreover, by common assent, it was *her* turn. So Sanders was starting at a pronounced disadvantage.

Yet the homegrown American socialist mounted a serious challenge to Clinton's preordained coronation, winning twenty-three primaries and amassing nearly nineteen hundred convention delegates.[4] For many young progressives, Bernie—the name itself conveying a down-home democratic aura, like Abe or Ike—became something of a rock star. Making this unexpected success all the more remarkable was the fact that the Democratic Party organization, abandoning any pretense of evenhandedness, tilted in Clinton's favor, exerting itself mightily to undermine Sanders's candidacy.[5]

As a campaigner, Bernie demonstrated a particular flair for connecting with younger voters. This suggested that Clinton's well-rehearsed got-everything-covered stance—in her commitment to the post–Cold War consensus, she was unyielding—was prompting a large number of Democrats to look for something different. Sanders was nothing if not different.

By veering from orthodoxy in a distinctly leftward direction, he earned votes and energized the young. "Feel the Bern" spoke to people in ways that Clinton's market-tested campaign slogan,

"Stronger Together," did not. Sanders was neither warm, nor fuzzy, nor particularly eloquent. Even so, he conveyed a sense of tell-it-like-it-is authenticity. Over many years in the national spotlight, Clinton had acquired an image of being cold, programmed, and perhaps phony, which she now struggled vainly to overcome. Despite looking like a Hollywood version of a slightly unkempt eccentric great-uncle, Sanders seemed by comparison like a fresh face.

That said, on issues related to culture and foreign policy, Sanders did not noticeably depart from conventional left-liberal views. He supported women's rights and gay rights. He denounced racism and xenophobia. He endorsed health care for all. On climate change he was a believer and on globalization a skeptic. He condemned the excessive militarization of U.S. policy and the misuse of American military power. Crucially, unlike then Senator Clinton, he had voted against the Iraq War.

Yet such matters figured only on the margins of his candidacy. A telephone conversation that I had with Sanders in February 2016, at the behest of his campaign staff, illustrates the point. After pelting me with various questions for perhaps fifteen minutes, he brusquely invited me to join a foreign policy advisory panel that his campaign was creating. Although I had never actually met Sanders, I agreed, if only because I judged every other candidate in the race somewhere between distasteful and repugnant.

I never heard from Sanders or his campaign again. To my knowledge, that advisory panel never formed. Here was one indication that for Bernie foreign policy qualified as an afterthought.

What Sanders cared passionately about was economic inequality and its myriad implications. "We must make our choice," Justice Louis Brandeis had once famously remarked. "We may have democracy, or we may have wealth concentrated in the hands of a few, but we can't have both."[6] Sanders shared this conviction. He believed further that unless Americans acted promptly and decisively, others would make that choice for them. In running for the presidency, Bernie was running against the very rich and their henchmen who, he was convinced, were actively engaged in obliterating American democracy.

So in a sense his campaign was monochromatic. At its core, it was all about the green—who had it and who didn't. A speech delivered at the Brookings Institution in 2015 captures the essence of his message to the American people.

Sanders had just visited the battlefield at Gettysburg. While driving back to Washington, he told his audience, "It struck me hard that Lincoln's extraordinary vision, a government of the people, by the people, for the people was, in fact, perishing, was coming to an end." In its place was emerging an "oligarchic form of society where today we are experiencing a government of the billionaires, by the billionaires, and for the billionaires."[7] Here was the theme to which he was to return again and again. Without economic democracy there could be no political democracy. Absent economic sufficiency for all, freedom was hardly more than a sham.

Sanders was by no means the first to make this argument. In January 1944, Franklin Roosevelt had used the occasion of his State of the Union address to propose what he called a "Second Bill of Rights" centered on ensuring basic economic security for all. "Necessitous men are not free men," the president declared. "True individual freedom cannot exist without economic security and independence."

Among the provisions he wanted included in his addendum to the original Bill of Rights was the right to "a useful and remunerative job" that paid enough "to provide adequate food and clothing and recreation," a right to a "decent home," medical care, and a "good education"; and a right to "adequate protection from the economic fears of old age, sickness, accident, and unemployment." In his peroration, Roosevelt declared, "All of these rights spell security." And without security at home, he insisted, there could not be peace abroad.[8]

During his run for the presidency, Sanders explicitly cited Roosevelt's 1944 State of the Union address as a model for his own reform agenda.[9] Yet for Sanders, there was this crucial difference: By 2016, the situation had become far more dire than during World War II.

After all, when Roosevelt spoke in 1944, American social cohesion was at an all-time high. And although the president could not have known it, the United States was then embarking upon a period in which sustained economic expansion actually served to enhance equality. During this "Great Compression," destined to last into the 1970s, the rich got richer, but low-income and middle-income Americans also benefited appreciably, enough to reduce the gap between the well-to-do and everyone else.[10]

By 2016, the Great Compression had long since given way to a Great Decompression. While the rich were still getting richer, most others struggled just to keep up. Meanwhile, social cohesion had seriously eroded.

None of this qualified as a secret. During the previous decade, economic discontent had inspired both the right-wing Tea Party and the left-wing Occupy Movement. Each created a stir without leaving much of a lasting mark. Until Sanders (and Trump) came along, protest was confined to the fringes, while the seemingly impervious juggernaut of globalized neoliberalism kept rolling on. Members of the political establishment saw no reason why it should not continue to do so indefinitely.

Yet as Sanders racked up victories in successive state primaries, jeopardizing Hillary Clinton's taken-for-granted nomination, it became increasingly difficult to dismiss him as a mere protest candidate and his supporters as a lefty fringe. Bernie's critique of what he called "casino capitalism" stirred the American electorate, generating energy and excitement that no other candidate in the race, regardless of party, could match—or at least no candidate but one.

The contrast between Sanders and Hillary Clinton in their head-to-head competition proved illuminating. No longer the closeted culture subversive she had been back in 1992 when she helped her husband win the presidency, Clinton embodied mainstream liberalism. In her own mind, she was a high-minded and forward-looking progressive with a realistic understanding of what it takes to govern. She saw Sanders as a wooly-headed fantasist given to making promises that in her eyes amounted to "little more than a pipe dream." After all, she had recruited, as she put it, "an experienced policy team with deep experience in government" along with "an extensive network of outside advisers drawn from academia, think tanks, and the private sector."[11] By contrast, Sanders had little more going for him than a stump speech.

Even so, it was Sanders who dictated the rhythm of the campaign to choose a Democratic nominee. He acted and Clinton reacted. Whenever she unveiled some new proposal, Clinton later wrote, "Bernie would come out with something even bigger, loftier, and leftier," not to mention, in the opinion of her expert advisers, more implausible. "That left me," she lamented, "playing the unenviable role of spoilsport schoolmarm, pointing out that there was no way Bernie could keep his promises."[12]

Given Clinton's perspective—politics providing the means to make incremental repairs to a flawed but essentially sound system—her frustration was understandable. Yet even after the campaign had ended, she failed to grasp how badly she had misread the moment. Whether or not his solutions were realistic, Sanders gauged the temper of the times far more accurately than had Clinton. The system itself was rigged, he charged. That's all that really mattered. Dismantling that system rather than tinkering with it, in his telling, had emerged as an urgent necessity. In 2016, here was a theme that could motivate voters.

The GOP Self-Destructs

Of all the movie action heroes who single-handedly dispatched a slew of demented enemies bent on their destruction, few if any have ever surpassed John Rambo. As played by Sylvester Stallone, Rambo was physically imposing and utterly fearless, even though haunted by his harrowing experiences while serving in the Vietnam War. Those experiences also imbued him with an acute sense of personal honor.

Yet the real key to his success in eliminating adversaries was the way that his opponents cooperated in arranging their own demise. However much they might outnumber and outgun Rambo, they obligingly presented themselves one at a time as targets to be picked off.

So it was in the race for the Republican nomination in 2016. No one would compare Donald Trump's stout figure with Stallone's well-sculpted physique. And unlike Rambo, Trump had no direct experience with war, whether actual or cinematic. As to honor, he possessed none, personal or otherwise. Even so, in the race to succeed Barack Obama, he became a Republican Rambo, picking off his rivals, more numerous than skillful, one at a time.

I will not test the reader's patience by trying to explain why Jim Gilmore (campaign slogan: "Gilmore for America") fancied that 2016 was his year to win the White House. The former governor of Virginia had last held office in 2002. His candidacy never got off the ground.

Something of the same applies to other retreads and wannabes who threw their hats in the ring, among them Chris ("Telling It Like It Is") Christie, the deeply unpopular outgoing governor of

New Jersey; George ("People over Politics") Pataki, the largely forgotten former chief executive of New York; and Mike ("Hope to Higher Ground") Huckabee, a former Arkansas governor turned right-wing pundit. Joining them in the long-shot category were Rand Paul, the chip-off-the-old-block libertarian senator from Kentucky, and Rick Santorum, the has-been former senator from Pennsylvania.

Add to that roster abortive efforts by Senator Lindsey Graham of South Carolina, former Texas governor Rick Perry, and two sitting governors, Bobby Jindal of Louisiana and Scott Walker of Wisconsin. Each of them ended his bid for the presidency without winning the support of even a single delegate.

In a different America at another time, Ohio governor John ("Kasich for Us") Kasich might have made a plausible Republican candidate. A moderate in the mold of Thomas Dewey, who had led the GOP to defeat in 1944 and again in 1948, Kasich was solid, seasoned, and sensible, even if possessing the charisma of a dozing mud turtle. These were not qualities that set hearts within the 2016 Republican rank and file aflutter. So although Kasich hung around for a while, his candidacy never caught fire.

Carly ("New Possibilities, Real Leadership") Fiorina had only recently arrived on the national political scene and was a woman to boot. In 1999, she had assumed the reins of Hewlett-Packard, becoming one of the few female CEOs of a Fortune top-twenty company. Yet HP's performance under her leadership proved less than stellar and in 2005 she was forced to resign. Five years later, she took a shot at winning a senate seat in California, but failed, leaving her in a position analogous to Richard Nixon's after he lost the gubernatorial race for that state in 1962. Yet when it came to engineering a comeback, Fiorina showed little of Nixon's political cunning. Although she weathered Donald Trump's insults—"Look at that face! Would anyone vote for that?"—her 2016 presidential candidacy ended abruptly when she won just 4 percent of the vote in the New Hampshire primary.[13]

Apart from Fiorina, Ben ("Heal. Inspire. Revive.") Carson was the only other Republican candidate who was not a white male. Like Fiorina, he was a novelty: a soft-spoken black social conservative and renowned neurosurgeon who had never held political office. Carson entered the race on May 4, 2015, and proved an effective fundraiser. Yet the novelty soon wore off. Failing to finish any higher than fourth in the eleven Super Tuesday Republican primaries, he ended his campaign on March 4, 2016, having spent $58 million of other people's money.[14]

In reality only three candidates stood a genuine chance of derailing the Trump juggernaut. Along with Jeb Bush, the former Florida governor and next in his family's dynastic line, there was Florida senator Marco Rubio and Texas senator Ted Cruz.

A single question haunted Jeb Bush's candidacy: Did he really want the job? His surname alone placed him in a rarefied circle. In all of American history, only four families had twice occupied the White House: First came John and John Quincy Adams, then William Henry and Benjamin Harrison, followed by the Roosevelts, Theodore and Franklin, and most recently the two George Bushes. For a third Bush to become president would put that clan in a league of its own.

Yet not every scion of a prominent political family feels a compulsion to compete for the top job. In 1979, as he contemplated a run for the presidency, Senator Edward Kennedy of Massachusetts revealed his ambivalence when on national television he appeared flummoxed by the question: "Why do you want to become president?"[15] Hamlet-like equivocation from a would-be commander in chief did not inspire confidence from the electorate.

Jeb Bush was the Teddy Kennedy of 2016, revealing a vulnerability that Donald Trump was quick to identify and exploit. "I think Jeb is a reluctant warrior," the real estate mogul volunteered even before announcing his own candidacy. "I actually don't think he wants to run. I watch him. I'm very good at reading people. I made a lot of money because I can read people. And when I watch Jeb Bush, he doesn't want to run. . . . He's not a happy guy. He's not enjoying it."[16]

Yet as the Republican establishment's preferred candidate, Bush emerged as the early front-runner. His campaign raised and spent an astounding $150 million.[17] Even as he burned through money at a prodigious rate without notable effect, irresolution emerged as his campaign's unspoken theme. As if to avoid calling attention to the fact that he and the by then deeply unpopular George W. Bush were siblings, his logo—"Jeb!"—skirted any mention of their shared last name.

Bush's equivalent to Kennedy's why-are-you-running gaffe came when he tied himself in knots trying to explain whether he supported his brother's decision to invade Iraq in 2003. By 2015, most observers, whatever their political affiliation, had come to see that decision as disastrously misguided. Yet asked point-blank during a *Fox News* interview in May of that year if he still supported the Iraq War, "knowing what we know now," Bush replied in the affirmative.[18]

When the answer elicited widespread scorn, even from fellow Republicans, he promptly backpedaled, claiming to have mis understood the question. While acknowledging that "there were mistakes in Iraq for sure," Bush now insisted that the issue of whether the invasion was right or wrong had become a mere hypothetical and so was not really worth revisiting.[19]

He never recovered from this misstep. Even before Super Tuesday, the candidate whom Trump disparaged as "low-energy Jeb" had bailed out of the race.

Senators Rubio and Cruz—in Trump-speak "Little Marco" and "Lyin' Ted"—had none of Jeb Bush's diffidence. They knew exactly why they wanted to be president. Ambition seeped from their pores like sweat on a racehorse.

Rubio ran as the self-appointed heir of Ronald Reagan. Cruz went Rubio one better. He ran as the self-designated heir of Jesus Christ. Present-day Republicans tend to remember Reagan's actual record selectively. Much the same applies to their adherence to Christ's teachings. In this regard, Rubio and Cruz did not disappoint.

Depicting Reagan as the best president in recent memory and Obama as the worst, Rubio used the Gipper's first successful presidential campaign as a prototype for his own effort in 2016. In effect, Rubio ran against Jimmy Carter—or against the image of Carter that Reagan had successfully contrived in 1980. Like Carter, Obama was weak. Like Carter, Obama had single-handedly and needlessly forfeited America's claim to global leadership. The antidote was principled assertiveness by a commander in chief who believed in the American mission.

Reagan had insisted (and Rubio concurred) that cutting taxes and government spending, eliminating burdensome regulations, and balancing the budget would guarantee prosperity in which all Americans would share. Yet Reagan's overarching message—designed to transcend differences in race, gender, ethnicity, and class—related to America's role in the world. Under Jimmy Carter, he contended, America had ceased to lead. Under a President Reagan, it would once again stand tall.

As a candidate in 1980, Reagan unveiled his intention to lead "a great national crusade to make America great again!" Prompting that crusade was a determination to reassert the country's global preeminence, lost due to Carter's "weakness, indecision, mediocrity and incompetence."[20]

In 2016, Rubio made Reagan's argument his own. Much as Reagan had corrected Carter's egregious blunders and brought the ship of state back on course, he pledged to undo Obama's mistakes.

"By abandoning this administration's dangerous concessions to Iran, and its hostility to Israel; by reversing the hollowing out of our military; by giving our men and women in uniform the resources, care and gratitude they deserve; by no longer being passive in the face of Chinese and Russian aggression; and by ending the near total disregard for the erosion of democracy and human rights around the world," Rubio promised to make things right. All that was needed, he insisted, was for the United States to don "the mantle of global leadership."[21] This he would personally do on the nation's behalf upon taking office.

In making such promises, Rubio seemed oblivious to all that had occurred since 9/11. So if his pitch had a familiar Reaganesque ring, it was also more than slightly off-key. Rubio vowed to lay the foundation for what he called a "New American Century." Yet in embracing this phrase, laden with connotations that were the very inverse of Donald Trump's revived use of "America First," he was tacitly aligning himself with the neoconservative "Project for a New American Century" that for years before 2003 had vociferously lobbied for the United States to depose Saddam Hussein.

As had Jeb Bush, Rubio tied himself in knots trying to answer the Iraq question, unable to justify yet unwilling to disavow his support for a preventive war that had gone badly awry.[22] More broadly, he seemed unaware of what the post–Cold War fervor for militarized hegemony had actually yielded in terms of gains and losses. Not since Herbert Hoover, who in running for reelection in 1932 bragged that a decade of Republican leadership had created unprecedented "standards of living and a diffusion of comfort and hope," had a presidential candidate been quite as tone-deaf as Marco Rubio.[23] Whether Hoover was dishonest or simply out of touch with reality was beside the point. He was obviously unsuited for the task at hand. So was Rubio.

For Trump, "Little Marco" offered an irresistible target. The senator from Florida, he charged, was "RobotRubio"—"just another Washington D.C. politician that is all talk and no action." He also had "really large ears, the biggest ears" that Trump had ever seen. And then there was the perspiration: "I have never seen a human being sweat like this man sweats."[24]

Insults of this sort (to which Rubio replied in kind) added appreciably to the entertainment value of the race for the nomination. Yet Trump's jeers did not sink Rubio's campaign. Rubio's candidacy expired of self-inflicted wounds.

Republican primary voters in 2016 did not want another crusade, any more than they wanted a repeat of the economic upheaval that had occurred the last time a Republican president came into office promising tax cuts and a balanced budget, only to deliver trillion-dollar deficits instead. They had had enough of banalities that, when put to the test, did not work as promised. They wanted a candid acknowledgment of the deficiencies inherent in the post–Cold War consensus. In short, they wanted something different and someone different. So when Rubio got clobbered in his own state's primary— Trump burying him by nearly twenty points—he was finished.

By mid-March 2016, only Ted Cruz stood between Donald Trump and the nomination. No one ever accused Senator Cruz of recording high marks on the likability scale. At a time when the bonds of bipartisanship had frayed to the point of disappearing, Senate colleagues on both sides of the aisle concurred on at least one point: Cruz was a total jerk. Lindsey Graham, a fellow Republican, suggested, "If you killed Ted Cruz on the floor of the Senate, and the trial was in the Senate, nobody would convict you."[25]

The Cruz persona struck some observers as altogether creepy. The writer Ben Fountain, covering the campaign for *Rolling Stone*, speculated that the senator "gargles twice a day with a cocktail of high-fructose corn syrup and holy-roller snake oil."[26] Yet as a candidate he left no doubt about where he stood: He was on God's side.

As *Chicago Tribune* columnist Steve Chapman wrote, the Cruz campaign all but identified him as "The Official Candidate of the Son of God."[27]

Chapman's jab made an essential point: Cruz did not present himself as the candidate of all God-fearing Americans regardless of their faith tradition. Instead, he identified his cause with that of conservative Christian evangelicals, a large and highly motivated segment of the Republican Party.

Not by accident, Cruz announced his candidacy before an audience of students at Liberty University, founded by the Reverend Jerry Falwell and presently the nation's largest Christian evangelical institution of higher learning. Some candidates wrap themselves in the flag; Cruz wrapped himself in a seamless garment that wove together God's purposes, American history, and the true meaning of freedom, with special emphasis on the Second Amendment.

"To God be the glory!" he proclaimed in February 2016 after eking out a victory in the Iowa caucuses.[28] The God whom Cruz sought to mobilize in support of his candidacy was specifically the Christian God. "If we awaken and energize the body of Christ," he assured his followers, "we will win and we will turn the country around."[29] On another occasion, he declared that "any president who doesn't begin every day on his knees isn't fit to be commander-in-chief."[30] The divine being to whom Cruz insisted presidents should direct their prayers was the one whose son was Jesus.

In effect, Cruz was training his fire on one particular element of the post–Cold War consensus. He did not oppose the further spread of corporate capitalism or America's pursuit of global hegemony enforced by superior U.S. military power. He certainly did not oppose sweeping presidential authority. But he did oppose what he saw as the perversion of freedom stemming from the abandonment of traditional Judeo-Christian norms. And he called for the restoration of those norms as the necessary antidote.

As a Republican electoral strategy, this was not without merit. What Cruz failed to anticipate was Trump horning in on issues that ought rightfully to have been his.

The thrice-married Trump, whose prior interest in religion had been negligible at best, refused to concede the conservative evangelical vote. Indeed, he courted evangelicals assiduously and with not inconsiderable success. Here was perhaps the most bizarre aspect of a uniquely bizarre presidential race.

While positioning himself to enter that race, Trump had pronounced himself a "very proud" Presbyterian and promised if elected president to be "the greatest representative of the Christians that they've had in a long time."[31] Nothing about Trump's life up to this point offered any reason to accept such a statement at face value.

Even so, in the contest to prove himself the more authentic supporter of old-timey Bible-based Christianity, he somehow came out on top. On the campaign trail, Cruz lambasted Trump as everything from a "sniveling coward" and "big loud New York bully" to a "pathological liar" and "serial philanderer." Trump was "utterly amoral," he charged.[32] While most of this was empirically correct, little of it made a lasting impression on conservative evangelical voters drawn to Trump. More than a few evangelical leaders joined Cruz in finding fault with Trump's character.[33] Yet the people in the pews tuned out these criticisms.

By 2016, conservative evangelicals were looking for a president who would pull down the Temple and rebuild it along lines more to their liking. Yet try as he might, Cruz could not disguise the fact that he made his living by working within the confines of that Temple. A sitting United States senator laboring to brand himself as a scourge of the Washington establishment, he was, in fact, part of the very system he professed to despise.

By comparison, Trump was indisputably an outsider. His bra-

vado, boundless self-confidence, and flair for devising impeccably simple solutions to seemingly insoluble problems—take the
oil, build the wall, drain the swamp—invested his antiestablish-
ment posturing with an apparent authenticity that Cruz was hard-
pressed to match.

So Trump got a pass from conservative evangelicals for much
the same reason that liberal feminists gave Bill Clinton a pass in
1992 and beyond, notwithstanding credible charges of sexual mis-
conduct. One particular White House correspondent had made the
point directly. "I would be happy to give [Clinton] a blowjob just
to thank him for keeping abortion legal," she remarked, adding
that "American women should be lining up with their Presidential
kneepads on to show their gratitude for keeping the theocracy off
our backs."[34] Liking the larger package, pro-Clinton feminists
were willing to overlook some unsavory details. Conservative evangelicals who accepted at face value Trump's unsubstantiated claim
of having been "born again" did likewise.[35]

Some evangelicals found in Scripture itself further confirmation that Trump might be well suited to serve as God's chosen
instrument. Chapter 45 of the book of Isaiah recounts the story of
Cyrus the Great, who although not believing in the Lord, delivers
the Israelites from the Babylonian captivity. That Trump might
do likewise, emancipating Christians from their twenty-first-
century Babylon, seemed to some believers eminently plausible.[36]

Put simply, members of the religious right saw Trump as a sinner
who could deliver on issues they considered of prime importance,
not least among them making abortion once more illegal. That
was evidently all they needed to hear.

In May 2016, Cruz admitted defeat and withdrew from the race.
After allowing the passage of just enough time to constitute a decent
interval—according to Cruz a period "of careful consideration, of

prayer and searching my own conscience"—the senator hoisted himself aboard the bandwagon and announced his support for Trump as president.[37]

Hillary Adflicta

So it came down to Trump versus Hillary Clinton. Only with trepidation do I venture to assess the Clinton candidacy in the presidential race of 2016. I did not vote for her. Neither, I hasten to add, did I vote for Donald Trump. Instead I joined the more than one hundred million Americans who preferred *other* or *none* to the nominees of the Republican and Democratic Parties.[38]

That Hillary Clinton was infinitely more qualified to serve as president than Donald Trump is inarguably the case. She had earned a shot at the top job in ways that Trump had not. She was a tested professional; he was a gate-crashing interloper, richly deserving of the invective to which he was subjected by members of his own party.

In my view, however, Clinton's very professionalism ended up hurting her more than it helped. True, whether as a candidate or a candidate's wife, whether as a senator or secretary of state, Clinton could be counted on to know her brief and to recite her lines. She worked very hard. Yet to many she managed to come across as either deeply cynical or morally obtuse.[39]

Politics as a profession has a sordid underbelly. It breeds a sense of entitlement and an absence of accountability. All too frequently, as people become accustomed to power, they exempt themselves from the rules to which the riffraff are expected to adhere. When things go awry, they are quick to give themselves a pass.

So it had been with Hillary Clinton long before she became her party's 2016 nominee. Despite being a professed feminist, she collaborated willingly in a concerted campaign to conceal her husband's sexual improprieties, both as a candidate for president and while he was in office. His ambitions and hers took precedence over their avowed support for gender equality and respect for women.

From her service in the 1980s on the board of Walmart, headquartered in the state where her husband was serving as governor, to her acceptance of high six-figure "honoraria" from investment banks just prior to her 2016 run for the presidency, Clinton was either oblivious to the appearance of influence peddling or assumed that such strictures did not apply to her. She expressed amazement that anyone would think that she could be bought.[40]

As a senator from New York, Clinton voted in favor of George W. Bush's prospective invasion of Iraq, parroting his administration's own rationale for preventive war.[41] While subsequently acknowledging that her vote had been a "mistake," in 2016 she spun that mistake into a claim that this earlier lapse in judgment had somehow put her in "the best possible position" to prevent the recurrence of another Iraq.[42] The debacle there had ostensibly taught her a lesson. Past folly apparently signified hard-won wisdom.

Yet her actions while serving as secretary of state during Barack Obama's first term belied that claim. In 2011, Clinton had pressed for armed intervention in Libya, nominally justified to prevent genocide, but actually intended to overthrow longtime Libyan strongman Muammar Gaddafi. On March 19, Western air attacks on the Gaddafi regime commenced. By October, the regime had collapsed and Gaddafi himself was dead. On national TV, a laughing Clinton bragged, "We came, we saw, he died."[43]

Yet liquidating Gaddafi no more settled the matter than the fall of Baghdad ended the Iraq War. His ouster merely paved the way for a years-long civil war. As Libya descended into anarchy, the United States largely washed its hands of further responsibility.

Years later, Clinton was still insisting that the intervention she had done so much to promote exemplified "smart power at its best," the apparent measure of merit being not the results achieved but the dearth of U.S. combat casualties.[44]

While secretary of state, Clinton also blatantly disregarded government policies pertaining to the handling of classified material. This egregious lapse allowed hackers to leak and subsequently post online tens of thousands of sensitive emails that she had sent and received.[45]

Clinton's cavalier attitude regarding the protection of state secrets testifies to her sense of entitlement. Yet to my mind, what made her unfit to serve as commander in chief were those decisions regarding Iraq and Libya. I found it difficult to escape the conclusion that political considerations had determined her vote for war in Iraq. After all, Democrats who had voted against the Iraq War of 1991 had had their presidential ambitions badly damaged. Even in 2002, no one doubted that she was angling for a shot at the White House. I also found her premature and unseemly victory dance regarding Libya indicative of someone possessed of a dangerously deficient understanding of war. On both counts, she became for me a figure not to be entrusted with executive responsibilities.

In short, on Iraq and Libya Clinton had committed mortal sins, for which I was not inclined to offer absolution, even were I empowered to do so. Would I be more forgiving if Clinton were a male, a Cheney, Rumsfeld, or Wolfowitz, for example? No. If the transgressions of Harvey Weinstein and others of his ilk merit perpetual obloquy, then feckless warmongering surely deserves no less, all gender considerations aside.

Clinton's penchant for misusing U.S. military power did not cost her the presidency in 2016. Yet it was emblematic of a larger problem: her adherence to the propositions informing the post–

Cold War outlook. Even taking into account the imperative of liberals tacking left during the primary season and back toward the center for the general election, nothing that Clinton said as a candidate suggested that she entertained second thoughts about the post–Cold War formula of globalized neoliberalism, militarized hegemony, radical autonomy, and presidential supremacy. In her campaign memoir, she lamented having "never quite shook the impression that I was the defender of the status quo." Yet that is precisely where she had positioned herself.[46]

To be sure, her commitment to that consensus was implicit rather than explicit. It was taken for granted rather than critically examined and forthrightly defended. Like most presidential candidates in recent years, Clinton smothered first-order questions in a barrage of promises that offered something for every imaginable constituency.

Her "comprehensive progressive vision for America's future" included the following: a reduced tax burden on working families; an end to the "quiet epidemic" of substance abuse; a cure for Alzheimer's disease; a "new, wide-ranging autism initiative"; campaign finance reform; the elimination of campus sexual assault; installation of a half billion solar panels to address climate change; the defeat of ISIS; criminal justice reform to terminate "the era of mass incarceration", expanded opportunities for the disabled; universal preschool for every four-year-old child; an end to the "epidemic of gun violence"; a gigantic infrastructure program; the eradication of HIV and AIDS; the elimination of child poverty; guaranteed paid family and medical leave; "universal, quality, affordable healthcare for everyone"; and a "safe and strong" America that will "lead the world in the 21st century."[47]

All this and more. Yet even this partial, if formidable, list begs the question: What was the underlying vision that informed Clinton's "vision"? Two answers to that question stand out.

First, Clinton's something-for-everyone set of promises represented the functional equivalent of Donald Trump's widely ridi-
culed claim, "Nobody knows the system better than me, which
is why I alone can fix it."[48] Clinton's campaign strategists assumed
that testifying to her own mastery of that system held one key to
electoral success. So whatever the problem, Clinton had readily at
hand her own plan to "fix it"—a chorus of dog whistles designed
to resonate with just about every group of potential supporters:
workers, women, the elderly, vets, people of color, gays, Jews, the
military-industrial complex, and even big business. Yet in marketing their competing "I alone" claims, both candidates were in
effect endorsing the post–Cold War paradigm of the U.S. president
as maximum leader and ultimate source of salvation.

Second, if Clinton's vision was stupefyingly grandiose, it was
also strikingly banal, its contents carefully vetted by Democratic
think tanks and pollsters. In the end, for all of Clinton's emphasis
on policy particulars, her vision amounted to little more than an
elaborate endorsement of the status quo. At root, hers was a tech-
nocratic program, constructed on the assumption that the principles governing the nation's political economy, guiding U.S. foreign
policy, and promoting cultural change were fundamentally sound.
As such, while they might require some adjustment to bring
them to perfection—a tad more emphasis here, a bit more money
there—there was no need to subject the principles themselves to
searching examination.

Such a perspective obviated any need to reflect seriously on whom
the post–Cold War project had injured, alienated, or left behind.
Clinton and the political establishment as a whole, not to mention
the agenda-policing mainstream media, took it for granted that the
injured, alienated, and left behind had no real option but to acqui-
esce and eventually get with the program.

Here lies the ultimate explanation for Clinton's inability to defeat her monumentally unqualified and ill-equipped adversary. Despite raising over $620 million, assembling a campaign staff ten times larger than Trump's, and recruiting a gaggle of policy experts to advise her, she not only failed to motivate the electorate, but conveyed a distinct cluelessness, as illustrated by her infamous dismissal of Trump's supporters as "deplorables."[49] Ironically, at least in his critique of globalization and of America's penchant for unnecessary wars (if not in his lip service to traditional moral norms), Trump managed to come across as both more forthright and more aware.

So blame Russian interference, FBI director James Comey, WikiLeaks, angry white males, and Clinton's failure to visit key swing states all you want. Her deepest problem was that she made herself the chief exponent of an existing policy consensus that large numbers of Americans were keen to discard. Elect me, she claimed in effect, and the Emerald City will be ours. But her argument assumed a pervasive gullibility that serial disappointments had long since converted into deep-seated anger.

Had Clinton rejected the inevitability of subsuming the American economy into a global market, questioned the pattern of U.S. military interventionism abroad, and ventured to suggest that the absence of individual self-restraint might not provide a sound basis for pursuing the common good, she might have come closer to exposing Trump as the charlatan he was. She might even have had a chance of winning over some of those who bought his "make America great again" agenda. But doing so would have required a capacity for critical imagination and independent thought that Clinton showed few signs of possessing.

All that said, give Trump his due. In the end, what won him the presidency was his capacity to push the buttons of millions of voters who believed themselves ill-served and left behind—abandoned even—by establishment politicians of both parties.

Implicit in his promise to make America great again was an admission that greatness itself, which Americans had long since come to believe was theirs by right, had been lost, with no one taking responsibility and no one, apart from Trump himself, venturing to explain how it had even happened. The critical word that imparted to his campaign slogan its formidable persuasive power was *again*. As Tom Engelhardt has written, it represented an acknowledgment that self-congratulatory terms such as "great," "super," "exceptional," or "indispensable" no longer reflected the actually existing American condition.[50] Millions of ordinary citizens recognized this as self-evidently true. Arrangements, agreements, and advantages that Americans had once prized had been squandered or thrown away. And yet no politician other than Trump dared to utter that truth aloud.

As a strategic thinker, Trump had no particular talent. Yet as a strategic *sensor*, he was uniquely gifted, possessing an intuitive genius for reading the temper of his supporters and stoking their grievances. Yet by no means did Trump create those grievances. They had festered during the quarter century after the Cold War ended. He merely recognized their existence and in doing so made himself the champion of the aggrieved and the one person they came to believe who might respond to their plight.

The election of 2016 constituted a plebiscite of sorts, the outcome turning less on the relative qualifications of the competing candidates than on the mood of the electorate. In effect, while Clinton was touting her plan for solar panels, Trump was transforming the election into a referendum centered on a single question: Are you satisfied with the direction in which the country is headed? Answer yes or no.

The number of pissed-off Americans responding to that question in the negative, their ranks effectively reinforced by the millions who did not vote at all, sufficed to install Trump in the White House. We may lament that outcome. Yet it is important to acknowledge that developments during the preceding quarter century had provided his supporters with ample motivation to vote as they did.

8

ATTENDING TO RABBIT'S QUESTION

For the multitudes counting on President Hillary Rodham Clinton to lead America onward to the Emerald City, the election of Donald Trump in her stead came as much more than a mere disappointment or even a shock. It was an intolerable affront. A great wrong had occurred. American democracy had gone off the rails. Dark forces had thwarted an outcome that was meant to be.

The reaction from those most protective of the post–Cold War outlook was instantaneous and severe. The opinion pages of the *New York Times*, long recognized as the nation's unofficial newspaper of record, but also the authoritative purveyor of enlightened opinion, offer a good sample of that reaction.

Collectively, the privileged platoon of *Times* columnists represented a model of twenty-first-century diversity: male and female, gay and straight, black and white, Jew and Gentile, proudly progressive and stoutly conservative. Yet when contemplating a prospective Trump presidency, they reached a unanimous conclusion: A disaster without precedent in U.S. history was about to befall the nation.

First out of the box on the very night of the election was an anguished Thomas Friedman, who with typical hyperbole declared himself "homeless in America."[1] Within a day, Maureen Dowd was writing that "the Apocalypse came at midnight," that being the hour when she realized that Trump's victory was certain and the world began "spinning off its axis."[2]

Dowd's colleague Gail Collins piled on, lambasting the new president-elect as dimwitted, mean-spirited, and "the spawn of Satan."[3] Frank Bruni foresaw nothing but disaster ahead. "I can't bear to think about the conflagrations to come," he wrote.[4] In that same edition of the *Times*, Roger Cohen concluded that "the world as we knew it is no more," even as he reassured himself that the United States was "not Weimar Germany."[5] Yet.

On the following day, it was Charles Blow's turn. "Trump represents a clear and very present danger," he asserted, while demanding that he be "placed under unrelenting pressure. . . . That begins today."[6] On November 11, David Brooks recounted the reaction of his family and friends to Trump's election. "This is victory for white supremacy," they told him, "for misogyny, nativism and authoritarianism. Fascism is descending." Brooks would by no means be the last columnist to bring the f-word into the conversation. Yet he consoled himself with the thought that "the guy will probably resign or be impeached within a year."[7]

On that same page, Paul Krugman predicted, "A Trump administration will do immense damage to America and the world." Nor would that damage be temporary. "Tuesday's fallout will last for decades, maybe generations."[8] Ross Douthat could only entreat his fellow conservatives to hold their noses and answer the call of duty, despite the president-elect's "hair-trigger temper, his rampant insecurity, [and] his personal cruelty." "Precisely *because* they fear how Trump might govern," he insisted, "there is a moral responsibility to serve."[9]

All this, before Trump had even named his first cabinet appointee. Even so, this flurry of denunciation merely hinted at what was to come. The media assault on Trump was just getting cranked up.

Between Trump's election and the end of his first year in office, for example, Charles Blow published eighty-eight columns in the *Times*, fifty-six targeting Trump specifically. Of the remainder, most tore into various reprobates who fleetingly passed through Trump's orbit, including Michael Flynn, Steve Bannon, Omarosa Manigault, and Anthony "The Mooch" Scaramucci. On those rare occasions when Blow refrained from going after Trump or his associates, he devoted himself to promoting the anti-Trump resistance, for which he served as a vocal cheerleader.

Throughout, Blow's tone was unremittingly contemptuous of the president and anyone in his employ. Trump, he wrote, was a bigot, fake, fraud, madman, degenerate, racist, and archenemy of truth. His presidency was tainted, parasitic, a menace, a horror, and an idiocracy. The president himself was the king of crash and burn, the chieftain of spite, and an insult to the intelligence of the average American.[10]

My point is not to take issue with these judgments, most of which, while overwrought, had considerable merit. Taken as a whole, however, Blow's obsession with Trump and his louche associates illustrates one of the most striking characteristics of the era: Simply by getting elected, Donald Trump prompted a large swath of the nation's most prominent gatekeepers to take leave of their senses. And not only journalists; members of the American intelligentsia followed suit. Within months of his taking office, Trump's most vociferous critics elevated him to the status of Caesar Augustus, Charlemagne, or Napoleon Bonaparte by declaring that a veritable "Age of Trump" had commenced. The president viewed himself as a world historical figure. Those who despised him most concurred.

Much as Osama bin laden had hijacked U.S. national security

policy in 2001, fifteen years later Donald Trump hijacked the principal organs of elite opinion, and with comparably unfortunate results. Following 9/11, senior U.S. national security officials effectively did bin Laden's bidding by embarking on a Global War on Terrorism that served his strategic purposes, while embroiling the United States in a series of open-ended and costly diversions that did nothing to advance the safety and well-being of Americans.

After 11/8, the *New York Times*, *Washington Post*, CNN, and MSNBC numbered among the institutions, both prominent and obscure, that suffered a nervous breakdown from which they did not wish to recover as long as Donald Trump remained in office. They effectively collaborated with the new president in transforming his misstatements, malapropisms, blatant untruths, and daily deluge of tweets into the central story of the age. This, too, proved to be a costly diversion.

So from a journalistic perspective, the Trump presidency was immeasurably worse—and therefore infinitely better—than Richard Nixon's had been. The scandals besetting Trump's administration were more varied, grotesque, and egregious than those filed under the heading of Watergate—and therefore made even better copy.[11] For journalists and members of the punditocracy, to live in a perpetual state of high dudgeon, denouncing Trump's latest inanity, charging him with treason, or likening him to Mussolini or Franco or Perón was to enjoy the equivalent of a protracted psychic orgasm, with the president himself as much partner as antagonist.[12]

Self-righteously posturing against Trump also proved good for business. It attracted readers and viewers. It sold books and magazines. It boosted TV ratings and drew eyeballs to websites. As television network executive Les Moonves remarked of Trump's arrival at the center of American politics, "It may not be good for America, but it's damn good for CBS." "The money's rolling in," he added, "and this is fun."[13]

It was a perverse conception of fun. Yet apart from the occasional natural disaster, mass shooting, terrorist incident, or sex scandal claiming the scalp of some Hollywood celebrity, archbishop, or New York powerbroker (soon including Moonves), President Trump did, in fact, dominate the nation's day-to-day collective consciousness as no figure ever had. Indeed, Trump's invariably ham-handed response to the latest devastating hurricane or massacre regularly attracted more press attention than the event itself. And his well-documented ill-treatment of women secured him a place at the very top of the #MeToo movement's Most Wanted list.

In short, even before Trump took the oath of office as president, he became the Great White Whale of the chattering classes.

Divided States of America

Obsessing about Trump impeded efforts to understand what his election actually signified, diverting attention from matters of far greater relevance to the well-being of the United States and the planet as a whole. Much the same could be said about Trump supporters, persuaded that their hero had the moxie and mojo to undo all the evils that a nefarious establishment had perpetrated in the years since the United States won the Cold War. They, too, attributed to the person of Donald Trump far greater significance than he merited.

This tacit alliance of anti- and pro-Trumpers thereby kept the focus riveted on the twenty-four-hour news cycle. In the Age of Trump, the American attention span shriveled, confined to the interval between last night's rants by Sean, Anderson, and Rachel and this morning's presidential tweets.[14] Foremost among the casualties resulting from this inclination were context and perspective.

On one point the two opposing camps seemingly agreed: Donald

Trump's conception of himself as a transformative figure deserved to be taken seriously. As a candidate, Trump vowed to change everything. As president, he was ostensibly doing just that, in the eyes of his supporters clearly for the better, to his critics with results somewhere between malign and simply evil.

It was Obama-mania turned inside out and magnified. When Barack Obama first won the presidency, his most fervent admirers—and they were legion—viewed him as akin to a messiah. Recall the massive crowds, cheering and weeping, gathered in Chicago's Grant Park on election night. Reporting from the scene, one journalist swooned, "The world has been hoping for Barack Obama for a long time." Now he had come. And with his arrival, "the divisiveness that the Bush administration and neo-conservatism fed on" had ended as, indeed, had the "long struggle for racial equality."[15] Poof. Just like that. Easy to mock in retrospect, this optimism was widespread. Rarely in the annals of American politics had emotions run so hot and hopes soared so high as they had in November 2008.

So it was with Trump, as well. When he won the election to succeed Obama, his most fervent critics—they, too, were legion—promptly castigated him as a secular Antichrist. Recall the "resistance" forces that gathered on the National Mall in Washington and in major cities across America to protest his inauguration. Here, too, emotions ran extraordinarily hot and high.

Expectations of Obama redeeming the nation—expunging the vestiges of racism and bringing an end to war, for example—never came to pass, as did fears of Trump leading Americans down the path to perdition. They, too, proved baseless and for the same reason: Even in the twenty-first century, history remained defiantly recalcitrant. Notwithstanding the apparently impervious American fixation with what presidents can, should, or must do, history does not bend to the whims of any individual, whatever their attributes and intentions.

It is, in fact, far too soon to proffer even a preliminary assessment of Trump's tenure as president. That statement will remain true whether Trump is gone from office before Election Day in 2020 or whether he somehow manages to win and complete a second term.

Yet the president's most ardent critics would have us believe otherwise. They are more than ready to hand down a definitive verdict, stoking fears of Trump ushering into existence a xenophobic white nationalist political order, the checks embedded in more than two centuries of constitutional rule thereby counting for naught. This prospect assumes that twenty-first-century America is indeed indistinguishable from Weimar Germany in the late 1920s and early 1930s.

Paradoxically, these same anti-Trumpers also assume that Trumpism itself will prove to be an epiphenomenon. Without Trump's active and ongoing leadership, it will shrivel up and die.

In sum, while Trump remains, all appears lost. Remove Trump and the march toward the Emerald City will promptly resume.

Such expectations betray a fundamental misreading of what the Trump presidency signifies. What the president's most prominent opponents have yet to appreciate is that the Emerald City consensus is as defunct as the Boone City consensus that preceded it.

The post–Cold War recipe for renewing the American Century has been tried and found wanting. A patently amoral economic system has produced neither justice nor equality, and will not. Grotesquely expensive and incoherent national security policies have produced neither peace nor a compliant imperium, and will not. A madcap conception of freedom unmoored from any overarching moral framework has fostered neither virtue nor nobility nor contentment, and won't anytime soon. Sold by its masterminds as a formula for creating a prosperous and powerful nation in which all citizens might find opportunities to flourish, it has yielded no such thing. This, at least, describes the conclusion reached by disenchanted Americans in numbers sufficient to elect as president someone vowing to run the post–Cold War consensus through a shredder.

Donald Trump's detractors commit this categorical error: They confuse cause and effect. They charge him with dividing America when, in fact, it was pervasive division that vaulted him to the center of American politics in the first place.

The divide is deepest and least reconcilable between those Americans for whom the trajectory of events since the Cold War pointed upward and those who found in those same events evidence of decline and decay and who sensed they'd been had. At the most fundamental level, the inhabitants of one camp believe that talent, skills, and connections will enable them to determine their own destiny; they are masters of their own fate. In the other camp are those who see themselves as victims. As Obama put it while campaigning for the presidency in 2008, "they cling to guns or religion or antipathy toward people who aren't like them or anti-immigrant sentiment or anti-trade sentiment as a way to explain their frustrations."[16]

Trump did not create this cleavage. He merely turned it to his personal advantage. So, regardless of the date or terms of Trump's departure from office, the schism that allowed him to become president is likely to persist after he is gone. It's that schism rather than the antics of the tycoon/reality TV star/demagogue who exploited it that merit far more attention than it has received.

Ours is a nation that is coming apart at the seams. The "mystic chords of memory" to which Abraham Lincoln once referred are stretched ever thinner.[17] Indeed, smartphones, Google, and Facebook make memory itself seem superfluous.

During several decades spanning the Great Depression, World War II, and the Cold War, Americans managed, though not without struggle, to maintain a tenuous and imperfect unity. Yet as the several crusades of the previous century fade into the past, it becomes increasingly difficult to discern what binds twenty-first-century Americans together as a people.

One thing certain is that they have had their fill of crusades. For confirmation, look no farther than abortive post-9/11 efforts to launch a new crusade targeting regimes in Iraq, Iran, and North Korea, the destruction of this "Axis of Evil" marketed as an essential next step toward fulfilling the nation's putative mission to spread freedom and democracy.[18] Outside of neoconservative circles, that effort never gained traction. By the time the Abu Ghraib scandal broke in April 2004, exposing the torture and abuse to which Iraqi detainees were being subjected by U.S. troops, it lost all remaining credibility.[19]

In the absence of crusades, what remains? Nearly unanimous disdain for Congress, vaguely patriotic rituals like singing the national anthem prior to sporting events, and lifestyle-related crazes like Black Friday and Cyber Monday cannot conceal what has become an ongoing process of fragmentation.[20] "Our tragedy," novelist Norman Mailer once wrote, "is that we diverge as countrymen further and further away from one another, like a space ship broken apart in flight which now drifts mournfully in isolated orbits, satellites to each other, planets none, communications faint."[21] If a half century premature, Mailer's diagnosis now turns out to be devastatingly accurate. Trump's election and the response that it evoked testify to this reality.

Making Sense of the Senseless

Considered as an episode in the ongoing history of the United States rather than as a sudden national nervous breakdown, what meaning can we assign to the Trump presidency, even if only on a tentative basis? Prevailing post–Cold War expectations and attitudes make that question all the more difficult to answer. After all, someone like Trump wasn't supposed to happen.

Yet with the passage of time an answer to that question will emerge. History is likely to judge Trump as somewhat less disruptive than he now appears (and wishes to appear) and as more of a transitory figure who simultaneously embodied and laid bare the accumulating contradictions of American life.

Note that most of the horrors predicted by Trump's critics have not come to pass—at least not as of this writing. The constitutional order remains intact. Press freedom has rarely been exercised with comparable vigor and passion. In the streets, ordinary citizens assemble, speak their minds, and raise their voices in protest. Those who are so inclined worship as they see fit. Despite frequent references to Fascism, that belief system remains distinctly unfashionable. Running for office as a Fascist is not a recipe for electoral success.

Indeed, one distinguishing attribute of the Trump presidency is the yawning gap between what the president vows (or threatens) to do and what in most cases actually ensues. Such a gap exists with any administration. With Trump, it reached unusually large proportions, exacerbated further by subversive subordinates.[22]

Recall the promises that energized candidate Trump's followers. He was going to revive American manufacturing and create millions of well-paying jobs for working stiffs. By cutting taxes, he would put lots more money in the average Joe's pocket. He was going to eliminate the trade deficit and balance the federal budget. He would end our endless wars and bring the troops home where they belong, while requiring America's freeloading allies to shoulder their share of the load. He would put a stop to illegal immigration. He would make the United States once more the God-fearing Christian country it was meant to be. All this together formed his vision of an America made great again.

Recall as well the button-pushing provocations that candidate Trump employed to incite establishment outrage, thereby delighting those holding that establishment in contempt. He promised to reauthorize torture and "load up" the U.S. military prison at Guantánamo "with some bad dudes."[23] He vowed to quit NATO, abandon the Iran nuclear deal, move the American embassy in Israel to Jerusalem, and jettison every trade deal that did not demonstrably benefit the U.S. economy. He would terminate Obamacare on "day one," appoint pro-life judges, and revive "Merry Christmas" as a holiday greeting. By unfurling the black banner of "America First," he implicitly subverted the foundational myth of contemporary history—World War II as a "Good War" that gave credence to America's providentially assigned liberating mission.

How seriously Trump himself expected any of those promises to be taken is anyone's guess. But this much is clear: Most remain unfulfilled. In those instances where what Trump said correlates with what his administration did, the results fell well short of apocalyptic.

True, after Trump became president, domestic manufacturing experienced a slight uptick. Yet globalization remained an implacable reality. Except for those with STEM degrees, good jobs were still hard to come by. Young hipsters might find the "gig economy" cool, but were likely to find it less so when reaching their sixties and wondering if they will ever be able to afford retirement.

While Trump and a Republican Congress did make good on their promise of tax "reform," its chief beneficiaries were the rich, further confirmation, if it were needed, that the American economy favors the few at the expense of the many.

As for the trade deficit, under Trump it hit a ten-year high.[24] Ending the flow of red ink was going to be easy, he had claimed. Instead of balancing the budget, his presidency brought a return to the trillion-dollar deficits of the Great Recession, boosting the national debt past $21 trillion.[25]

While the Republican Party retained control of the Senate, President Trump enjoyed considerable success in appointing conservative judges to the bench. This raised ire among progressives, especially his nomination of Brett Kavanaugh to the Supreme Court. Even so, although never to be taken for granted, the rule of law remains in reasonably good shape.

Trump did keep his promises to pull out of the Iran nuclear deal and move the U.S. embassy from Tel Aviv to Jerusalem, something that Israeli governments and the domestic Israel lobby had been promoting for decades. I was not alone in fearing that each of these could have dangerously destabilizing effects. I need not have worried. Little of substance changed.

Despite U.S. withdrawal from the Joint Comprehensive Plan of Action, Iran and the other signatories to the agreement remained in full compliance with its terms.[26] If Trump's action was intended to provoke the Iranian government into some action that could be construed as a casus belli, as Iranophobes clearly hoped, it failed. As for planting the U.S. embassy in Jerusalem and then recognizing Israeli sovereignty over the Golan Heights, these actions merely substantiated already existing, if seldom acknowledged, truths: The "two-state solution" is a fiction; in the dispute between Israelis and Palestinians, Washington in no sense plays the role of honest broker; in matters affecting Israel, the national interests of the United States figure as an afterthought.

And then there was the great bugaboo of "isolationism." When Trump became president, various foreign policy experts predicted that the United States was about to turn its back on the world and abandon its self-assigned role as keeper of order and defender of democracy. Yet isolationism is the last word one would use to characterize foreign policy since Trump became president.

Today, the United States remains formally committed to defending the territorial integrity of each and every NATO member state, now numbering twenty-nine in all. Add to that a continuing obligation to defend various other nations, including Japan, South Korea, and, under the terms of the Rio Pact of 1947, most of Latin America. Less formally but no less substantively, the United States ensures the security of Israel, Saudi Arabia, and various other countries in the Persian Gulf. Whatever the inspiration of Trump's weird bromance with Vladimir Putin, the Pentagon clearly views Russia as a threat, as evidenced by the growing U.S. military presence in Poland and the Baltic republics.[27]

As for cracking down on allied free riding, as Trump had insisted he would do, that never made it past the rhetorical stage. America's European allies, for example, pocketed Trump's assurances that the United States will continue to defend them, offering in return vague promises that sometime around 2024 they might consider investing more in defense. That promise elicited from the self-proclaimed master negotiator the laughable statement that "NATO is much stronger now than it was two days ago."[28]

Meanwhile, despite various minor drawdowns, U.S. forces under Donald Trump's ostensible command remained present in three-fourths of the world's independent nations.[29] After briefly flirting with possible cuts, Trump reversed course and backed a further boost of the Pentagon budget for 2020.[30] Without bothering to check first with senior U.S. military leaders, Trump himself promised to create a new branch of the armed services—a "Space Force" intended to dominate outer space itself, a goal, according to the president, that is "important for the nation's psyche."[31]

Whatever this motley collection of initiatives adds up to, the result conforms to no plausible definition of isolationism.

As for the promised barrier sealing the southern border, the president struggled to advance that project beyond the display of possible prototypes. Zero evidence suggested that Mexico would cover the cost of erecting a "big, fat, beautiful wall," as Trump had insisted it would. Indications that the U.S. Congress will appropriate the necessary funds—estimated at somewhere north of $20 billion—were hard to find, and became more so after Republicans lost control of the House of Representatives in November 2018.[32] Under President Trump, the U.S.-Mexico border remained what it had been for decades: patrolled but porous, a conduit for desperate people seeking safety and opportunity, but also for criminal elements trafficking in drugs, weapons, and human beings.

And, of course, America's wars did not end. After more than a year in office, Trump was still claiming that he was "constantly reviewing Afghanistan and the whole Middle East," while reiterating his conviction that U.S. military involvement in that region "was the single greatest mistake in the history of our country."[33]

That judgment came closer to being indisputably true than just about any other statement of Trump's presidency. Even so, through his first two years in office, Trump had sustained and in some instances escalated America's military interventions in the Islamic world, even while essentially insulating himself from responsibility for their perpetuation.[34] That Trump wanted to lower the U.S. military profile in the Greater Middle East was no doubt the case. Yet in his efforts to do so, he met fierce resistance from the foreign policy establishment and from members of the officer corps sworn to follow his orders.

Truth to tell, as commander in chief, Trump took a hands-off approach. He did not immerse himself in the details of military policy. He rarely consulted directly with his field commanders or visited U.S. troops serving abroad. Despite being unable to walk, Franklin Roosevelt spent more time with GIs serving in combat zones.

Finally, Trump came nowhere close to inaugurating the moral revival that his conservative evangelical base apparently expected. With Trump in the White House, Americans might be at liberty to say "Merry Christmas" in preference to "Happy Holidays," but the ongoing displacement of formal religion from the public square showed no signs of abating. The tide of secularization continued to rise, unaffected by anything that the nation's philanderer in chief said or did.

By these measures and others, Trump's America did not differ appreciably from pre-Trump America. While a noxious and venal blowhard, the president turned out not to be the disruptive force that his critics charged him with being.

So if only to control their blood pressure, Americans would do well to disregard the atmospherics—the lies and invective, the posturing and braggadocio. Through the first three years of Trump's tenure in the Oval Office, the basic fabric of American life emerged largely intact. Nor is it likely that the president will damage that fabric appreciably, regardless of when and under what circumstances he finally leaves office. That said, the widely held sense that the election of Donald Trump represents a turning point of sorts is not without foundation. It's just that his critics misconstrue what that turn connotes.

Himself a mountebank of the very first order, Trump exposed as fraudulent the triumphalism that served as a signature of the post–Cold War decades. On this score, Trump mattered and bigly.

With Trump in the White House, claims that the fall of the Berlin Wall inaugurated an era of American political, economic, military, and cultural ascendancy became impossible to sustain. In fact, End-of-History boosterism, backed by the conviction that America had perfected a system of political economy, mastered war, and discerned the true meaning of freedom, has turned out to be utterly wrongheaded, doing untold damage to Americans and others. The genius of Trump's "Make America great again" campaign slogan derived from its implicit admission that assertions of greatness made in the wake of the Cold War had turned out to be both empty and perverse.

From Exploitation to Eclipse

Our inflated post–Cold War view of the presidency makes it diffi-cult for Americans to consider this possibility: that Trump is play-ing only a minuscule part in a tragedy unfolding on a grand scale. In effect, he is a mere bit player.

Imagine, in fact, Trump and Hillary Clinton as contemporary equivalents of Rosencrantz and Guildenstern in Shakespeare's *Hamlet*. In that play, the two courtiers function as pawns in a drama they do not begin to comprehend. Much the same can be said of Trump and Clinton. In the 1960s, the playwright Tom Stoppard famously transformed Rosencrantz and Guildenstern into comic fig-ures. It took the writers on *Saturday Night Live* to do the same with The Donald and Hillary. Notably, while advancing the plot, Shakespeare's throwaway characters do not determine its outcome. Neither will the forty-fifth president and the woman who so des-perately wanted his job. Shakespeare's play turns on the fate of Hamlet, not on that of the expendable Rosencrantz and Guildenstern. What matters at present is not the fate of Donald Trump, who is likewise expendable.

While the principal themes of *Hamlet* are murder and revenge, the principal themes of the tragedy in which Donald Trump briefly appears are vanity and blindness—and not his alone. To an extent still not fully appreciated, the animating spirit of the post–Cold War era centered on the prospect of exploitation, taking advantage of the favorable circumstances in which the United States found itself—and which Americans claimed credit for creating. After all, with the fall of Communism, the way seemed clear to create a global order privileging American ideas and cementing the advan-tages enjoyed by at least some Americans, perhaps in perpetuity.

Unfortunately, during the interval between 1989 and 2016, Americans were blindsided by events that contravened such expectations. Unforeseen problems eroded the advantages that the end of history had ostensibly conferred. Exploitation produced not advantage, but eclipse.

That eclipse has taken three forms. First, the era of Western primacy, with the United States as the ultimate successor to once-formidable European empires, has now ended for good. The emergence of China as a global superpower offers only the most obvious indication of this reality. No less important is the fact that belief in the inherent superiority of Western civilization—taken for granted as recently as the middle of the last century—has now become politically and morally unacceptable. And with good reason: To suggest that Western values and culture are to be preferred, say, to Asian values or Islamic culture bears an indelible taint of racism.

Second, the era in which the benefits of technological advance necessarily outweigh any negative consequences is now winding down. Tech produces speed, efficiency, and precision, along with two qualities especially prized by Americans, namely, convenience and an antidote to boredom. Yet these benefits exact a price that includes submission to vast, profit-hungry corporate entities. Lurking in the near future, as smart machines become too smart for our own good, is the potential for lost jobs and the irretrievable loss of privacy.

Third, the era in which "taming" nature translates directly into human benefit has now run its course. Climate change, with all its myriad aftereffects, testifies to this development. But there are other indicators, ranging from massive deforestation to the accumulation of plastic waste in the oceans and from the decimation of bird populations to the collapse of bee colonies. Simply put, the way that humankind in the twenty-first century aspires to live is pushing Earth to the brink of exhaustion.

These issues will define the balance of the twenty-first century: an eastward shift of global power; technological dystopia; and potentially irreversible environmental degradation. To none of these does neo-liberal globalization, the pursuit of militarized hegemony under the guise of global leadership, and freedom defined as the removal of limits provide anything even approximating an adequate response. Quite the opposite.

All the Pilgrims

Take these perplexing challenges into account and Rabbit Ang-strom's bleak question acquires renewed urgency: What exactly, then, is the point of being an American?

Some observers may bridle at the question's implied premise. Perhaps today there is no more point to being an American than to being a Canadian. After all, citizens of Canada get along just fine without fancying themselves called upon to save the world or remake it in their own image. Yet for centuries now Americans have been conditioned to see themselves as uniquely anointed. They will not easily shed this aspect of their self-identity.

From John Winthrop to Ronald Reagan, leaders speaking in a prophetic register have articulated, affirmed, and expanded upon the American mission to usher the world's pilgrims onward toward some Promised Land. In their day, Thomas Jefferson, Abraham Lincoln, Woodrow Wilson, Franklin Roosevelt, and John F. Kennedy returned again and again to this theme, their sentiments echoed by innumerable orators reciting patriotic sentiments on Memorial Day, the Fourth of July, and comparable occasions. America's obligation to lead and liberate has long since insinuated itself into the DNA of the nation's political elite.

Even nonbelievers in such circles persist in assuming that Americans are a Chosen People, called upon to effect God's purposes on earth. They consider irrelevant the fate befalling other nations that once entertained a comparably grandiose sense of mission—

just in the twentieth century their ranks included Great Britain, France, Germany, Japan, and the Soviet Union. So to suggest that the necessary antidote to Trump might be for the United States to content itself with being a nation more akin to the depleted Britain of Elizabeth II than to the ambitious England of Elizabeth I is unlikely to fly, especially among those who covet power. After all, you don't get far up the greasy pole of politics by donning a cloak of humility and promulgating puny proposals.

So American politics will almost surely remain a forum for hyperbolic promises. Candidate Trump understood this full well. Hence, the shrewdness of his vows to drain the swamp, build the wall, end the carnage, and so on ad nauseam.

Perhaps the answer to Rabbit's question, if there is one, might be found in realigning that traditional sense of mission with current conditions. When the Cold War ended, American elites had their chance to do just that and failed miserably. They misread the conditions and propagated a set of deeply flawed policies.

Seduced by the perception that history had reached its intended conclusion, members of that elite persuaded themselves that neoliberalism implemented on a planetary scale, an approach to global leadership centered on the use or threatened use of armed force, and the abandonment of individual self-restraint—all of this unfolding under the aegis of presidents able to decipher the signs of the times—would deliver humankind to the Emerald City of prosperity, peace, and perfect freedom. Among that city's residents, they fully expected Americans to enjoy more than their fair share of the benefits, as was their due.

Yet the results of a quarter-century-long experiment in implementing the post–Cold War consensus turned out to be grotesque inequality, seemingly perpetual war, anomie on an epidemic scale—and Donald Trump. If the end of history in 1989 installed America in a commanding position, then someone screwed up royally. To charge President Trump with responsibility for that screwup is to indulge in the sort of scapegoating and buck-passing that Trump himself raised to a fine art.

Even today, despite all that has occurred since, evidence that the elites who devised those policies are willing to reckon with the extent of their failure is sparse. If anything, Trump provides a made-to-order excuse for further deferring any such reckoning. Anyone counting on members of the policy elite to acknowledge the scope of their collective failure is in for a long wait.

How, then, to devise an adequate answer to Rabbit's question? To begin with, it might be worth enlarging the scope of the discussion. It's past time to reconsider propositions that in recent decades have been deemed out of bounds. Perhaps heresies deserve a second look.

Among their least attractive qualities, proponents of the post–Cold War outlook did not welcome dissent. To reject globalized neoliberalism was to be labeled either a socialist or an economic Neanderthal. To question Washington's growing propensity for armed interventionism abroad was to be charged with being an isolationist, a declinist, or, worst of all, antimilitary. To wonder if unbounded libertinism might create its own forms of imprisonment was to risk being denounced as either intolerant or a killjoy. To suggest that the concentration of power in the Oval Office was both imprudent and at odds with the Constitution was to invite the charge of being simply naive.

The unsettling presidency of Donald Trump suggests that the time might be ripe for introducing into the conversation ideas previously classified as beyond the pale. Reframing the conversation on economic policy, America's role in the world, the meaning of freedom, and, not least of all, the distribution of political power, particularly in Washington, just might point toward a fresh understanding of the nation's purpose.

After all, Trump's rejection of the post–Cold War vision of an open world policed by the armed forces of the United States earned him the presidency. His own personal and professional life prior to becoming president testifies to the emptiness of even the cushiest form of liberty when untethered from any larger moral purpose. And his performance in office exposes once and for all the folly of elevating one person to the status of Supreme Leader.

Yet the immediate need is not to impose a new consensus, but to allow serious debate. In a country as deeply divided as the United States, the proximate aim should not be to obscure differences but to sharpen them further and thereby give them meaning. Americans deserve choices that go beyond Trump vs. Clinton or Republicans vs. Democrats or what currently passes for conservative vs. what gets labeled progressive.

Real debate about real choices would allow for the possibility of some alternative to globalized neoliberalism and the inequality that it produces—for example, an economy based on stewardship rather than satisfying an ever-growing appetite for consumption. It would reject militarized hegemony as a fantasy and reassess the reliance on so-called volunteers to fight never-ending wars. It would consider the possibility of freedom entailing obligations as well as rights. Finally, it would examine the wreckage caused by abandoning the concept of a federal government consisting of three coequal branches.

The existing political establishment has no incentive to promote or even permit any such debate. Nor do any of the other centers of power in twenty-first-century America, including the national security apparatus, the military-industrial complex, Wall Street, Silicon Valley, and the Washington "swamp" that candidate Trump once vowed to drain. They all benefit from the status quo and are devoted to perpetuating its well-oiled mechanisms for bestowing wealth, status, and privilege on the few while withholding them from the many. So real debate conducive to genuine change is unlikely to come from above.

Yet the past offers assurances that real change is possible. Previous chapters in U.S. history suggest that it occurs when the American people rally around a large cause that obliges officeholders to take note or be sent packing. One such cause was abolition, which started a train of events culminating in an immense conflict that destroyed slavery. The abuses suffered by American workers as a direct result of late nineteenth-century industrialization provided the basis for another such cause, this one yielding the wide-ranging reforms of the Progressive movement. Perhaps more familiar today is the Great Depression, an economic calamity that inspired the New Deal and war-induced sequels, like the GI Bill. In each instance, a morally grounded cause laid the basis for a new consensus with transformative implications.

A comparable cause presents itself today, even if obscured by Trump Derangement Syndrome. That cause is climate change. Evidence that climate change poses a clear and present danger continues to mount, a point driven home by the accumulation of once-in-a-century weather events.[35] Even the Pentagon sees the warming planet as a problem (an example of Trump's subordinates disregarding the boss).[36] What the Pentagon has yet to acknowledge is that the threat posed by climate change already exceeds the threat posed by Islamic terrorism and will eventually surpass that of Kim Jong-un's North Korea, Ayatollah Ali Khamenei's Iran, Vladimir Putin's Russia, or even Xi Jinping's China, none of them, it should be noted, exempt from that very same threat.

Future generations will rightly condemn Trump's inaction in the face of this looming crisis—indeed, for exacerbating it by dismantling environmental protections, promoting continued reliance on fossil fuels, and offering aid and comfort to science deniers. Yet however reprehensible, policy changes implemented at Trump's behest did not represent a fundamental departure from the past. In 1992, prior to the first Earth Summit in Rio de Janeiro, President

George H. W. Bush reputedly declared, "The American way of life is not up for negotiation."[37] None of his successors dared to repudiate that assertion. As a result, Washington's response to climate change ever since has tended to be cautious and incremental.

So when Miami is underwater and California wildfires rage year-round, Americans are unlikely to single out Trump for blame. The truth is that a succession of administrations share responsibility for the nation's too little, too late response to climate change. Their failure, abetted by Congress, illustrates precisely the trivializing paralysis of the post–Cold War outlook. Declaring an end to history inhibited efforts to focus attention on the surprises history still had in store.

Sooner or later, Americans will come to the realization that climate change is making their way of life unsustainable. Citizens may then discover that any serious effort to alleviate its impact will necessarily require adoption of an economic model that prizes fairness and equity above share prices and quarterly profit statements. In addition, they may choose to forgo "wars of exhaustion" in favor of a less militarized and more enlightened approach to global leadership.[38] They might even embrace a conception of citizenship that seeks to harmonize individual freedom with the common good. In sum, the imperative of addressing climate change may one day offer a suitable replacement for the disastrously misguided consensus foisted on the American people after the fall of the Berlin Wall. Here, in sum, are the makings of a suitable answer to Rabbit Angstrom's question.

That Donald Trump is oblivious to all of this goes without saying. Yet such matters may lie beyond any president's purview. When all is said and done, presidents don't shape the country; the country shapes the presidency—or at least it defines the parameters within which presidents operate. Over the course of the last few decades, in our headlong quest to reach the Emerald City, those parameters have become increasingly at odds with the collective well-being of the American people, not to mention of the planet as a whole.

Considered in retrospect, it becomes apparent that the fall of the Berlin Wall did not mark the "end of history." Nor did it constitute a turning point in the history of the United States. It merely removed the brakes, accelerating processes already well advanced. The end of the Cold War promised the fulfillment of a distinctly American version of modernity. Donald Trump's ascent to the presidency testifies to the abject failure of that project.

"The great error of our nature," wrote Edmund Burke in 1756, "is not to know where to stop" and thereby ultimately "to lose all we have gained by an insatiable pursuit after more."[39] This single sentence captures the essence of the fate that has befallen Americans during the quarter century following the Cold War.

What destination awaits us in the near future is difficult to know. It won't be Boone City or the Emerald City and it certainly won't be the City of God. What we can say with some confidence is this: In a nation ostensibly of, by, and for the people, ultimate responsibility for recognizing the need to change rests with those people. For Americans to shirk that responsibility will almost surely pave the way for more Trumps—or someone worse—to come.

NOTES

INTRODUCTION

1. John Updike, *Rabbit at Rest* (New York: Knopf, 1990), 367.
2. The remark, which survives in various forms, is attributed to Georgi Arbatov, founder and director of the Institute for the U.S. and Canadian Studies at the Russian Academy of Sciences. Jean Davidson, "UCI Scientists Told Moscow's Aim Is to Deprive U.S. of Foe," *Los Angeles Times* (December 12, 1988).

1. AL, FRED, AND HOMER'S AMERICA—AND MINE

1. The War Department and Navy Department had planned for demobilization to occur over a period of two to three years. Instead, the process unfolded in helter-skelter fashion over a mere nine months. From October 1945 to February 1946, more than three-fourths of a million service personnel returned to civilian life each month. By June 30, 1946, "demobilization had been virtually completed," with the total population of military veterans having increased by more than 12.8 million. General Omar Bradley, Administrator of Veterans Affairs, *Annual Report for Fiscal Year Ending June 30, 1946* (Washington, D.C., 1947), 1.
2. *The Best Years of Our Lives* (1946), directed by William Wyler. Dana Andrews played the part of Fred Derry.

3. Robert Warshaw, "The Anatomy of Falsehood," *Partisan Review* (Summer 1947), 305.

4. John Foster Dulles, "Thoughts on Soviet Foreign Policy and What to Do About It," *Life* (June 10, 1946).

5. For a canonical assertion of this proposition, see "NSC 68: United States Objectives and Programs for National Security" (April 14, 1950), https://www.mtholyoke.edu/acad/intrel/nsc-68/nsc68-1.htm, accessed June 26, 2017.

6. C. Wright Mills, *The Power Elite* (New York, 1956); Daniel J. Boorstin, *The Image: A Guide to Pseudo-Events in America* (New York, 1962); Christopher Lasch, *The Culture of Narcissism: American Life in an Age of Diminishing Expectations* (New York, 1978).

7. Steve Eder and Dave Phillips, "Donald Trump's Draft Deferments," *New York Times* (August 1, 2016). Some evidence suggests that a friendly podiatrist, who rented a property owned by Trump's father, may have helped his landlord's son avoid being conscripted. Steve Eder, "Did a Queens Podiatrist Help Donald Trump Avoid Vietnam?" *New York Times* (December 26, 2018).

8. For a concise overview, see Ken Hughes, "Richard Nixon: Domestic Affairs," Miller Center, https://millercenter.org/president/nixon/domestic -affairs, accessed October 27, 2017.

9. Paul Lewis, "Nixon's Economic Policies Return to Haunt the G.O.P.," *New York Times* (August 15, 1976).

10. Ronald Reagan, "Remarks Announcing Candidacy for the Republican Presidential Nomination" (November 13, 1979); "Address Accepting the Presidential Nomination at the Republican National Convention in Detroit" (July 17, 1980).

11. Ronald Reagan, "Inaugural Address" (January 20, 1981).

12. Ronald Reagan, "Farewell Address to the Nation" (January 11, 1989).

13. An image of the ad is available at https://www.buzzfeed.com/ilanbenmeir /that-time-trump-spent-nearly-100000-on-an-ad-criticizing-us?utm _term=.dhXAnvnL6#.wdRK878aR, accessed October 28, 2017.

14. In December 1988, a month prior to Reagan leaving office, polls indicated that 63 percent of Americans approved of his job performance, with just 29 percent disapproving. "The American Presidency Project: Presidential Job Approval," http://www.presidency.ucsb.edu/data/popularity.php?pres =40, accessed October 29, 2017. In 1988, Trump bought the Taj Mahal casino in Atlantic City, New Jersey, the storied Plaza Hotel adjacent to

Central Park, and the Eastern Airlines Shuttle, which he renamed the Trump Shuttle. All three proved to be money losers.

15. George H. W. Bush, "Inaugural Address" (January 20, 1989).

2. THE END OF HISTORY!

1. *Soviet Military Power: An Assessment of the Threat, 1988* (Washington, D.C., 1988), 8–13. This publication, prepared by the Office of the Secretary of Defense, appeared annually during the 1980s.

2. Reinhold Niebuhr, *The Irony of American History* (New York: Scribner, 1952), 3, 71.

3. For a summary of Trump's achievements and disappointments in the 1980s, see Michael Kranish and Marc Fisher, *Trump Revealed: An American Journey of Ambition, Ego, Money, and Power* (New York: Scribner, 2016), chapters 7–10.

4. Glenn Plaskin, "The People's Billionaire," *New York Daily News* (February 26, 1989).

5. Barbara Ehrenreich, *The Worst Years of Our Lives: Irreverent Notes from a Decade of Greed* (New York: Pantheon, 1990).

6. Gary Smith, "Donald Trump," *People* (October 4, 1989).

7. https://www.youtube.com/watch?v=fK1MwhEDjHg; https://www.youtube.com/watch?v=y-9_uQx6IsQ, accessed July 4, 2017.

8. Tom Shales, "The Day the Wall Cracked," *Washington Post* (November 10, 1989).

9. https://www.youtube.com/watch?v=snsdDb7KDkg, accessed July 4, 2017.

10. https://www.youtube.com/watch?v=BjZ2z0mNGvI, accessed July 4, 2017.

11. https://www.youtube.com/watch?v=mU4g0HOqxTk, accessed July 4, 2017.

12. Tom Wicker, "Decline of the East," *New York Times* (November 14, 1989).

13. Serge Schmemann, "Clamor in the East; Germans' Special Time," *New York Times* (November 16, 1989).

14. "After the Wall," *New Republic* (December 4, 1989).

15. George H. W. Bush, "Remarks and a Question-and-Answer Session with Reporters on the Relaxation of East German Border Controls" (November 9, 1989).

16. Rowland Evans and Robert Novak, "NATO Troop Withdrawals? No," *Washington Post* (November 13, 1989).

17. Walter S. Mossberg and Robert. S. Greenberger, "Policy Void: Upheaval in Europe Tests Bush's Capacity for Leadership of West," *Wall Street Journal* (November 14, 1989).

18. Mary McGrory, "Berlin and Bush's Emotional Wall," *Washington Post* (November 14, 1989).

19. William F. Buckley, "Capitulation in Peking," *National Review* (February 28, 1972).

20. For an important and underappreciated accounting, incorporating both second thoughts and sober reflection, see Derek Leebaert, *The Fifty-Year Wound* (New York, 2002).

21. Alfred Thayer Mahan, "The United States Looking Outward," *Atlantic* (December 1890).

22. Frederick Jackson Turner, "The Significance of the Frontier in American History" (1893).

23. Rudyard Kipling, "The White Man's Burden" (1899).

24. Francis Fukuyama, "The End of History?" *National Interest* (Summer 1989).

25. "X" [George F. Kennan], "The Sources of Soviet Conduct," *Foreign Affairs* (July 1947).

26. Walter Lippmann, *The Cold War: A Study in U.S. Foreign Policy* (New York: Harper, 1947). For an excerpt, see https://www.learner.org /workshops/primarysources/coldwar/docs/lippman.html, accessed July 12, 2017.

27. See, for example, this account of Kennan dissenting from policies ostensibly originating in Kennan's own prescriptions: Marvin Kalb, "The Vital Interests of Mr. Kennan," *New York Times Magazine* (March 27, 1966).

28. Quoted in James Atlas, "What Is Fukuyama Saying? And To Whom Is He Saying It?" *New York Times Magazine* (October 22, 1989).

29. "Responses to Fukuyama," *National Interest* (Summer 1989).

30. Strobe Talbott, "The Beginning of Nonsense," *Time* (September 11, 1989).

31. For contemporaneous synopses of that debate, see Henry Allen, "The End. Or Is It? Francis Fukuyama and the Schism over His Ism," *Washington Post* (September 27, 1989); and Richard Bernstein, "The End of History, Explained for the Second Time," *New York Times* (December 10, 1989).

32. Francis Fukuyama, "After Neoconservatism," *New York Times Magazine* (February 19, 2006).

3. KICKING 41 TO THE CURB

1. For a colorful contemporaneous account of Trump's troubles, see Marie Brenner, "After the Gold Rush," *Vanity Fair* (September 1990).
2. Russ Buettner and Charles V. Bagli, "How Donald Trump Bankrupted His Atlantic City Casinos, but Still Earned Millions," *New York Times* (June 11, 2016).
3. Bush's postpresidential memoir, coauthored with his national security adviser, simply ignored domestic issues altogether. George Bush and Brent Scowcroft, *A World Transformed* (New York: Knopf, 1998).
4. Chris Whipple, *The Gatekeepers: How the White House Chiefs of Staff Define Every Presidency* (New York: Crown, 2017), 163. The comic strip appeared in the week of November 3, 1984.
5. http://www.presidency.ucsb.edu/data/popularity.php?pres=41, accessed February 5, 2018.
6. George H. W. Bush, "Address Before a Joint Session of the Congress on the Persian Gulf Crisis and the Federal Budget Deficit" (September 11, 1990).
7. Franklin D. Roosevelt, "State of the Union Address" (January 6, 1941).
8. Ronald Reagan, "Address Accepting the Presidential Nomination at the Republican National Convention in Detroit" (July 17, 1980).
9. George Bush, "Remarks Accepting the Presidential Nomination at the Republican National Convention in Houston" (August 20, 1992).
10. Bill Clinton, "A New Covenant for Economic Change," Georgetown University (November 20, 1991).
11. Patrick J. Buchanan, "Address to the Republican National Convention" (August 17, 1992).
12. "Pat Buchanan for President 1992 Campaign Brochure," http://www.4president.org/brochures/1992/patbuchanan1992brochure.htm, accessed January 13, 2018.
13. Patrick Buchanan, "A Crossroads in Our Country's History," Concord, New Hampshire (December 10, 1991).
14. Kevin Sack, "Perot Ready to Start Using Short TV Commercials," *New York Times* (October 8, 1992).
15. Perot infomercial on the economy (October 6, 1992), https://www.youtube.com/watch?v=hzHugbDvKC4, accessed March 15, 2019.

16. The transcripts of the 1992 presidential debates appeared in the *New York Times* on October 12, 16, and 20, 1992.

17. Maureen Dowd, "Hillary Clinton as Aspiring First Lady: Role Model, or a 'Hall Monitor' Type?," *New York Times* (May 18, 1992).

4. GLIMPSING THE EMERALD CITY

1. L. Frank Baum, *The Wonderful Wizard of Oz* (Chicago: George M. Hill Company, 1900), 110.

2. Neil Postman, *Technopoly: The Surrender of Culture to Technology* (New York: Knopf, 1992).

3. Thomas Friedman, *Longitudes and Attitudes* (New York: Farrar, Straus and Giroux, 2002), 3; "Globalization: The Super Story," https://genius .com/Thomas-friedman-globalization-the-super-story-annotated.

4. Roland Robertson, *Globalization: Social Theory and Global Culture* (Thousand Oaks, California, 1992), 8.

5. The phrase is attributed to Marshall McLuhan, reflecting in 1968 on the proliferation of electronic media. "Today electronics and automation make mandatory," he wrote, "that everybody adjust to the vast global environment as if it were his little home town." Marshall McLuhan and Quentin Fiore, *War and Peace in the Global Village* (New York, 1968), 12.

6. William Graham Sumner, *The Forgotten Man and Other Essays* (New Haven, Connecticut, 1879 [rpt. 1919]), 215.

7. On the former, see Alfred W. Crosby Jr., *The Columbian Exchange: Biological and Cultural Consequences of 1492* (Westport, Connecticut, 1972).

8. Thomas L. Friedman, "A Manifesto for a Fast World," *New York Times Magazine* (March 28, 1999).

9. Alan Tooze, "Beyond the Crash," *Guardian* (July 29, 2018).

10. Benjamin R. Barber, "Jihad vs. McWorld," *Atlantic* (March 1992).

11. Between 1988 and 2001, annual U.S. military spending in constant dollars decreased from $587 billion to $418 billion. https://www .sipri.org/sites/default/files/Milex-constant-2015-USD.pdf, accessed August 26, 2017.

12. In 1990, U.S. military spending amounted to 37.1 percent of the world total. In the ensuing years, it increased to over 40 percent. https://howmuch.net/articles/military-spending-around-the-world, accessed August 26, 2017.

13. Michael Cooper, "C.I.A. Secrets Illuminate the Cold War," *New York Times* (December 4, 1994).

14. William James, "The Moral Equivalent of War" (1910).

15. These include several wars fought against the French at England's behest prior to 1776; innumerable campaigns against Native Americans; the war against the "Barbary pirates"; wars fought after 1898 to suppress Filipino nationalists and pacify the "Moro Province"; the Boxer Rebellion; and multiple interventions in Mexico and throughout the Caribbean during the first third of the twentieth century.

16. Colin L. Powell, "U.S. Forces: Challenges Ahead," *Foreign Affairs* (Winter 1992/1993).

17. For a useful primer, see Gary Chapman, "An Introduction to the Revolution in Military Affairs," XV Amaldi Conference on Problems in Global Security (September 2003), http://www.lincei.it/rapporti/amaldi/papers/XV-Chapman.pdf, accessed April 21, 2018.

18. *Joint Vision 2010* (1996), http://webapp1.dlib.indiana.edu/virtual_disk_library/index.cgi/4240529/FID378/pdfdocs/2010/Jv2010.pdf, accessed April 21, 2018.

19. James Davison Hunter, *Culture Wars: The Struggle to Define America* (New York: Basic Books, 1991), 43–44.

20. "Text of Eisenhower Speech," *New York Times* (December 23, 1952). Eisenhower had spoken the previous evening to the Freedoms Foundation in New York City.

21. "Message to the National Co-Chairmen, Commission on Religious Organizations, National Conference of Christians and Jews" (July 9, 1953).

22. Will Herberg, *Protestant, Catholic, Jew* (Chicago: University of Chicago Press, 1984 [rpt]), 84.

23. Raymond Aron, *The Opium of the Intellectuals* (Paris: Calmann-Lévy, 1955).

24. "Remarks of Senator John F. Kennedy Announcing His Candidacy for the Presidency of the United States" (January 2, 1960).

25. David Margolick, "Blair's Big Gamble," *Vanity Fair* (June 2003).

26. Maureen Dowd, "Immersing Himself in Nitty-Gritty, Bush Barnstorms New Hampshire," *New York Times* (January 16, 1992).

27. John F. Kennedy, "Annual Message to the Congress on the State of the Union" (January 30, 1961).

28. The best-known complainant was the historian Arthur Schlesinger Jr., sycophantic chronicler of the Kennedy family, whose disgust with

President Richard Nixon prompted him to write *The Imperial Presidency* (Boston, 1973).

29. Charles E. Wolcott and Karen M. Hult, "White House Staff Size: Explanations and Implications," *Presidential Studies Quarterly* (September 1999).

5. BEDFELLOWS

1. The election of 1964 was the exception that proves the rule. Barry Goldwater was not an establishment-approved candidate. His epic defeat persuaded the Republican Party never again to nominate a candidate who strayed from the mainstream.
2. William J. Clinton, "Inaugural Address" (January 20, 1993).
3. For an account of this episode, see Nathan J. Robinson, "The Death of Ricky Ray Rector," *Jacobin* (November 5, 2016).
4. Bill Clinton, "Remarks on Signing the North American Free Trade Agreement Implementation Act" (December 8, 1993).
5. Bill Clinton, "Remarks on Signing the Gramm-Leach-Bliley Act" (November 12, 1999).
6. Bill Clinton, *My Life* (New York: Knopf, 2004), 859.
7. Stephen F. Cohen, *Failed Crusade: America and the Tragedy of Post-Communist Russia* (New York: W. W. Norton, 2001).
8. For an English-language translation of bin Laden's text, see https://ctc.usma.edu/app/uploads/2013/10/Declaration-of-Jihad-against-the-Americans-Occupying-the-Land-of-the-Two-Holiest-Sites-Translation.pdf, accessed February 19, 2018.
9. Clinton, *My Life*, 955.
10. "Week 24: Ask Backwards," *Washington Post* (August 15, 1993).
11. "1999: Major Stories of the Year," ABC News (December 29, 1999).
12. Donald J. Trump with Dave Shiflett, *The America We Deserve* (Los Angeles, 2000).
13. Interview with Chris Matthews, *Hardball,* MSNBC (November 18, 1999).
14. Interview with Sean Hannity and Alan Colmes, *Hannity and Colmes,* Fox News (October 7, 1999).
15. Accompanying compassion was wariness about anyone expecting a free ride. "It is compassionate to actively help our fellow citizens in need," Bush later explained. "It is conservative to insist on responsibility and on results." George W. Bush, "Address on Compassionate Conservatism" (April 30, 2002).

16. Presidential Debate in Winston-Salem, North Carolina (October 11, 2000).

17. Woodrow Wilson, "Address to the Congress on International Order" (February 11, 1918).

18. Walter Lippmann, *Interpretations, 1931–1932* (New York, 1932), 262.

19. Derek Leebaert, *Magic and Mayhem* (New York, 2010), 283n3.

20. Joel Roberts, "Plans for Iraq Attack Began on 9/11," *CBS News* (September 4, 2002), https://www.cbsnews.com/news/plans-for-iraq-attack-began-on -9-11/, accessed July 21, 2018.

21. "Bush Defends Embattled Rumsfeld," BBC News (April 18, 2006).

22. George W. Bush, "Speech to Congress" (September 20, 2001).

23. George W. Bush, "Graduation Speech at West Point" (June 1, 2002).

24. George W. Bush, "Speech to Congress" (September 20, 2001).

25. George W. Bush, "Second Inaugural Address" (January 20, 2005).

26. John Yoo, "The President's Constitutional Authority to Conduct Military Operations Against Terrorists and Nations Supporting Them" (September 25, 2001). Yoo was then serving as deputy assistant attorney general in the Department of Justice.

27. http://www.nme.com/features/every-time-donald-trump-has-appeared -on-saturday-night-live-2019406, accessed May 22, 2018.

28. *The Situation Room,* CNN (March 16, 2007).

29. During President Bush's first term, Rice served as national security adviser. In 2005, she succeeded Colin Powell as secretary of state.

30. Kimberly Amadeo, "U.S. Debt by President: By Dollar and Percent," *Balance* (April 13, 2018).

31. "The Nobel Peace Prize for 2009," https://www.nobelprize.org/nobel _prizes/peace/laureates/2009/press.html, accessed June 5, 2018.

32. Scot Paltrow, "In Modernizing Nuclear Arsenal, U.S. Stokes New Arms Race," Reuters (November 21, 2017).

33. www.icasualties.org, accessed June 6, 2018.

34. F. Brinley Bruton, "U.S. Bombed Iraq, Syria, Pakistan, Afghanistan, Libya, Yemen, Somalia in 2016," *NBC News,* https://www.nbcnews.com /news/world/u-s-bombed-iraq-syria-pakistan-afghanistan-libya-yemen -somalia-n704636, accessed June 7, 2018.

35. John Haltiwanger, "Under Trump, U.S. Military Deaths in War Zones Are Up for the First Time in Six Years," *Newsweek* (November 20, 2017).

36. "Obergefell v. Hodges," *Oyez,* https://www.oyez.org/cases/2014/14-556, accessed June 8, 2018.

37. "A Profound Ruling Delivers Justice on Gay Marriage," *New York Times* (June 26, 2015).
38. Catherine Elsworth, "Barack Obama: 'Marriage Is Between a Man and a Woman,'" *Telegraph* (November 3, 2008).
39. "Transcript: Obama's Remarks on Supreme Court Ruling on Same-Sex Marriage," *Washington Post* (June 26, 2015).
40. Reinhold Niebuhr, *The Irony of American History* (New York, 1952), 71, 79, 91.
41. *The Laura Ingraham Show* (March 20, 2011), https://www.youtube.com/watch?v=WqaS9OCoTZs, accessed June 10, 2018.
42. "President Obama Roasts Donald Trump at White House Correspondents' Dinner" (April 30, 2011), https://www.youtube.com/watch?v=k8TwRmX6zs4, accessed June 10, 2018.

6. STATE OF THE UNION

1. Bill Scher, "Newsflash: It's Going to Be Hillary vs. Jeb," *Politico* (May 31, 2015).
2. U.S. Census Bureau, *2012 Census of Governments.*
3. F. Scott Fitzgerald, "The Rich Boy," *Red Book* (January and February 1926).
4. Katie Sola, "Here Are the States with the Most Billionaires," *Forbes* (March 5, 2016).
5. Chase Peterson-Whithorn, "Donald Trump Falls 35 Spots on the Forbes 400," *Forbes* (October 4, 2016).
6. Lawrence Mishel and Jessica Scheider, "CEO Pay Remains High Relative to the Pay of Typical Workers and High-Wage Earners," *Economic Policy Institute* (July 20, 2017).
7. "What Is the Current Poverty Rate in the United States?" *Center for Poverty Research* (December 18, 2017). In the population with incomes below the poverty line, 18.5 million lived in "deep poverty," defined as having a household income below 50 percent of the official poverty threshold.
8. Justin McCarthy, "Economy Continues to Rank as Top U.S. Problem," Gallup (May 16, 2016), https://news.gallup.com/poll/191513/economy-continues-rank-top-problem.aspx, accessed June 25, 2018.
9. Center on Budget and Policy Priorities, "Chart Book: The Legacy of the Great Recession" (June 5, 2018), https://www.cbpp.org/research/economy/chart-book-the-legacy-of-the-great-recession, accessed

June 25, 2018. One factor contributing to the drop in unemployment statistics was the fact that some Americans simply gave up looking for work. During the Great Recession, the labor participation rate dropped from 66 percent to less than 63 percent. Bureau of Labor Statistics, "Labor Force Statistics from the Current Population Survey" (June 26, 2018), https://data.bls.gov/timeseries/LNS11300000, accessed June 26, 2018.

10. Bureau of Labor Statistics, "Unemployment Holds Steady for Much of 2016 but Edges Down in the Fourth Quarter" (March 2017), https://www.bls.gov/opub/mlr/2017/article/unemployment-holds-steady-for-much-of-2016-but-edges-down-in-fourth-quarter.htm, accessed June 25, 2018.

11. Matt Egan, "America's 7-Year Bull Market: Can It Last?" *CNN Money* (March 9, 2016).

12. Lindsay Dunsmuir, "U.S. Fiscal Year Budget Deficit Widens to $587 Billion," Reuters (October 14, 2016); Federal News Network, "White House Budget Breakdown: FY 2016 Agency-by-Agency Funding Levels" (February 2, 2015), https://federalnewsnetwork.com/budget/2015/02/white-house-budget-breakdown-fy-2016-agency-by-agency-funding-levels/, accessed June 27, 2018.

13. Drew Desilver, "5 Facts About the National Debt," Pew Research Center (August 17, 2017).

14. Sarah A. Donovan and David H. Bradley, "Real Wage Trends, 1979–2017," *Congressional Research Service* (March 15, 2018).

15. Ben Casselman, "Manufacturing Jobs Are Never Coming Back," *FiveThirtyEight* (March 18, 2016), https://fivethirtyeight.com/features/manufacturing-jobs-are-never-coming-back/, accessed June 27, 2018.

16. Michael D. Carr and Emily E. Weimers, "The Decline in Lifetime Earnings Mobility in the U.S.: Evidence from Survey-Linked Administrative Data," Washington Center for Equitable Growth (August 2016).

17. Kathleen Elkins, "Here's How Much the Average US Family Has in Credit Card Debt," *CNBC Make It* (May 17, 2017).

18. Kathleen Elkins, "Here's How Much the Average American Family Has Saved for Retirement," *CNBC Make It* (September 12, 2016).

19. Monique Morrissey, "The State of American Retirement," Economic Policy Institute (March 3, 2016).

20. Todd Campbell, "Americans' Average Social Security Benefit at Age 66," *The Motley Fool* (December 16, 2016).

21. Max Kutner, "The Number of People on Food Stamps Is Falling.

Here's Why," *Newsweek* (July 22, 2017); United States Department of Agriculture Economic Research Service, "National School Lunch Program" (March 15, 2018), https://www.ers.usda.gov/topics/food-nutrition-assistance/child-nutrition-programs/national-school-lunch-program.aspx, accessed June 26, 2018; U.S. Department of Housing and Urban Development, *The 2016 Annual Homeless Assessment Report (AHAR) to Congress* (November 2016).

22. Hugo Martin, "Universal Studios Raises Ticket Prices Just Before It Opens New Harry Potter Attraction," *Los Angeles Times* (March 23, 2016).

23. "Stats: 24.7 Million Passengers Took Cruise in 2016, Says CLIA," *Travel Agent Central* (May 23, 2017), https://www.travelagentcentral.com/cruises/stats-24-7-million-passengers-took-cruise-2016-says-clia, accessed June 27, 2018; Jennifer Wood, "A Record Number of Americans Traveled Abroad in 2016," *The Points Guy* (January 4, 2017), https://thepointsguy.com/2017/01/record-number-of-americans-traveled-abroad-2016/, accessed June 27, 2018.

24. "The World's Biggest Gamblers," *Economist* (February 9, 2017); Derek Thompson, "Lotteries: America's $70 Billion Shame," *Atlantic* (May 11, 2015).

25. Neal Gabler, "The Secret Shame of Middle-Class Americans," *Atlantic* (May 2016).

26. Michael Paulson, "'Hamilton' Raises Ticket Prices: The Best Seats Will Now Cost $849," *New York Times* (June 8, 2016).

27. Wick Sloane, "Veterans at Elite Colleges, 2016," *Inside Higher Ed* (November 11, 2016). Columbia University, and to a lesser extent Georgetown, are honorable exceptions to this abysmal record of admitting undergraduate veterans.

28. Douglas L. Kriner and Francis X. Shen, "Invisible Inequality: The Two Americas of Military Sacrifice," *University of Memphis Law Review* 46 (2016): 545–635.

29. David M. Halbfinger and Steven A. Holmes, "A Nation at War: The Troops; Military Mirrors a Working Class America," *New York Times* (March 30, 2003).

30. Tom Vanden Brook, "Army to Spend $300 Million on Bonuses and Ads to Get 6,000 More Recruits," *USA Today* (February 12, 2017).

31. *Planned Parenthood v. Casey*, 505 U.S. 833 (June 29, 1992).

32. Sara G. Miller, "1 in 6 Americans Take a Psychiatric Drug," *Scientific American* (December 13, 2016).

33. National Institute of Mental Health, "Major Depression" (November 2017).

34. Substance Abuse and Mental Health Services Administration, *Reports and Detailed Tables from the 2016 National Survey on Drug Use and Health* (May 17, 2018).

35. CDC, "Opioid Overdose" (October 23, 2017).

36. CDC, "Alcohol and Public Health" (May 10, 2018).

37. National Center for Health Statistics, "Suicide Rates in the United States Continue to Increase" (June 2018); CDC, "Suicide Rates for Teens Aged 15–19 Years, by Sex—United States, 1975–2015" (August 4, 2017).

38. "15 Terrifying Statistics on Your Cellphone Addiction," http://www.dailyinfographic.com/15-terrifying-statistics-about-cell-phone-addiction, accessed July 3, 2018.

39. Mallory Schlossberg, "6% of Americans Are Affected by an Uncategorized Disorder That Involves Compulsive Shopping," *Business Insider* (December 10, 2015); Sara Solovitch, "Hoarding Is a Serious Disorder—and It's Only Getting Worse in the U.S.," *Washington Post* (April 11, 2016).

40. Eating Disorder Hope, "Eating Disorder Statistics and Research," https://www.eatingdisorderhope.com/information/statistics-studies, accessed July 3, 2018.

41. CDC, "Overweight and Obesity" (November 24, 2017).

42. American Society of Plastic Surgeons, *Plastic Surgery Statistics Report 2016*, https://www.plasticsurgery.org/documents/News/Statistics/2016/plastic-surgery-statistics-full-report-2016.pdf, accessed July 4, 2018.

43. Webroot, "Internet Pornography by the Numbers: A Significant Threat to Society," https://www.webroot.com/us/en/resources/tips-articles/internet-pornography-by-the-numbers, accessed July 3, 2018

44. CDC, "Reported STDs in the United States, 2016" (September 2017).

45. American Psychological Association, "Marriage and Divorce," http://www.apa.org/topics/divorce/, accessed July 4, 2018.

46. Claudio Sanchez, "Poverty, Dropouts, Pregnancy, Suicide: What the Numbers Say About Fatherless Kids," *NPR Ed* (June 18, 2017).

47. U.S. Department of Health and Human Services, *Child Maltreatment 2015* (Washington, D.C., 2017).

48. CDC, "Reproductive Health" (November 16, 2017).

49. "U.S. Leads World in Firearms Ownership," *Boston Globe* (June 19, 2018).

50. Christine Hauser, "Gun Death Rate Rose Again in 2016, C.D.C. Says," *New York Times* (November 4, 2017).

51. Prison Policy Initiative, "States of Incarceration: The Global Context 2016" (June 16, 2016).

52. Ana Swanson, "Americans Are Less Trusting Than Ever Before," *Washington Post* (August 26, 2016).

53. Pew Research Center, "U.S. Trails Most Developed Countries in Voter Turnout" (May 21, 2018).

54. "Social Isolation, Loneliness Could Be Greater Threat to Public Health Than Obesity," *Science Daily* (August 5, 2017).

55. Jessica Boddy, "The Forces Driving Middle-Age White People's 'Deaths of Despair,'" *NPR Shots* (March 23, 2017).

56. Nicholas Bakalar, "U.S. Fertility Rate Reaches a Record Low," *New York Times* (July 3, 2017).

57. Adam Chandler, "Why Americans Lead the World in Food Waste," *Atlantic* (July 15, 2016); Justin Gillis and Nadja Popovich, "The U.S. Is the Biggest Carbon Polluter in History," *Los Angeles Times* (June 1, 2017); Ann M. Simmons, "The World's Trash Crisis, and Why Many Americans Are Oblivious," *Los Angeles Times* (April 22, 2016).

58. Reef Karim, "Tattoo Psychology: Art or Self Destruction? Modern-Day Social Branding," *Huffington Post* (January 9, 2013).

59. Pew Charitable Trusts, "Explosion in Tattooing, Piercing Tests State Regulators" (June 14, 2017), http://www.pewtrusts.org/en/research-and-analysis/blogs/stateline/2017/06/14/explosion-in-tattooing-piercing-tests-state-regulators, accessed July 4, 2018.

60. Amy Wang, "The World Happiness Report Is Out and the U.S. Has Fallen. Sad!," *Washington Post* (March 20, 2017).

7. PLEBISCITE

1. GovTrack, "2016 Report Card: All Senators," https://www.govtrack.us/congress/members/report-cards/2016/senate/ideology, accessed July 17, 2018.

2. Edward-Isaac Dovere, "Sanders Had Big Ideas but Little Impact on Capitol Hill," *Politico* (March 12, 2016).

3. Paul Kane and Philip Rucker, "An Unlikely Contender, Sanders Takes on 'Billionaire Class' in 2016 Bid," *Washington Post* (April 30, 2015).

4. "Democratic Party presidential primaries, 2016," *Wikipedia,* accessed July 22, 2018.

5. Michael D. Shear and Matthew Rosenberg, "Released Emails Suggest

the D.N.C. Derided the Sanders Campaign," *New York Times* (July 22, 2016).

6. Quoted in Raymond Lonergan, "A Steadfast Friend of Labor," in Irving Dillard, ed., *Mr. Justice Brandeis, Great American* (St. Louis: Modern View Press, 1941), 42.

7. Brookings Institute, "An Economic Agenda for America: A Conversation with Senator Bernie Sanders" (February 9, 2015), https://www.brookings.edu/wp-content/uploads/2015/01/20150210_sanders_economic_agenda_transcript.pdf, accessed July 28, 2018.

8. Franklin Roosevelt, "State of the Union Message to Congress" (January 11, 1944).

9. Bernie Sanders, "Speech at Syracuse, New York" (April 12, 2016), https://www.youtube.com/watch?v=G3W9SthxzsI, accessed July 30, 2018.

10. Claudia Goldin and Robert A. Margo, "The Great Compression: The Wage Structure of the United States at Mid-Century," National Bureau of Economic Research (August 1991).

11. Hillary Rodham Clinton, *What Happened* (New York: Simon & Schuster, 2017), 224, 230.

12. Ibid., *227*.

13. Jessica Estepa, "Donald Trump on Carly Fiorina: 'Look at That Face!'," *USA Today* (September 10, 2015).

14. "Super Tuesday Results 2016," *New York Times* (March 1, 2016).

15. https://www.youtube.com/watch?v=b6qLFAnBIFg, accessed August 6, 2018. The correspondent posing the question was Roger Mudd of CBS News.

16. Matt K. Lewis, "Does Jeb Bush Even Really Want to Be US President?" *{London} Telegraph* (May 16, 2015).

17. Alicia Adamczyk, "How Much Money Failed Presidential Candidates Have Blown Through This Election," *Money* (February 21, 2016).

18. https://www.youtube.com/watch?v=Sie83xAmLkQ, accessed August 6, 2018.

19. Ed O'Keefe and Robert Costa, "On Iraq Question, Jeb Bush Stumbles and the GOP Hopefuls Pounce," *Washington Post* (May 13, 2015).

20. Ronald Reagan, "Republican National Convention Speech" (July 17, 1980). For a Reagan campaign "Let's Make America Great Again" campaign poster, see https://www.iagreetosee.com/portfolio/make-america-great-again/, accessed August 14, 2018.

21. "Transcript: Read Full Text of Sen. Marco Rubio's Campaign Launch," *Time* (April 13, 2015).

22. Leslie Hunter and Hunter Walker, "Marco Rubio Seems to Have Changed His Mind About the Iraq War," *Business Insider* (May 13, 2015).

23. Herbert Hoover, "Campaign Speech in Madison Square Garden" (October 21, 1932).

24. Tessa Berenson, "Here Are Trump and Rubio's Best Schoolyard Insults," *Time* (March 1, 2016).

25. Catherine Treyz, "Lindsey Graham Jokes About How to Get Away with Murdering Ted Cruz," *CNN Politics* (February 26, 2016).

26. Ben Fountain, *Beautiful Country Burn Again: Democracy, Rebellion, and Revolution* (New York: Ecco, 2018), 47.

27. Steve Chapman, "Are Ted Cruz and Marco Rubio Running for President or Pastor?," *Chicago Tribune* (February 3, 2016).

28. Sarah Posner, "Ted Cruz Has Mastered the Art of Evangelical Politics," *Week* (February 3, 2016).

29. Esther Laurie, "Ted Cruz: 'Awaken and Energize the Body of Christ,'" *Church Leaders* (February 4, 2016).

30. Nick Wing, "Ted Cruz: An Atheist 'Isn't Fit to Be' President," *Huffington Post* (November 9, 2015).

31. Leonardo Blair, "Donald Trump Tells Christians 'I'm Presbyterian' and 'Proud of It,'" *Christian Post* (June 22, 2015).

32. Madeline Conway, "9 Times Ted Cruz Insulted Donald Trump Before Endorsing Him," *Politico* (September 23, 2016).

33. Jack Jenkins, "A List of Faith Leaders Calling Out the Religious Right for Failing to Abandon Trump," *Think Progress* (October 9, 2016).

34. Howard Kurtz, "A Reporter with Lust in Her Heart," *Washington Post* (July 6, 1998).

35. Trip Gabriel and Michael Luo, "A Born-Again Donald Trump? Believe It, Evangelical Leader Says," *New York Times* (June 25, 2016).

36. See, for example, Kobena Charm, *Is Donald Trump America's Cyrus the Great?* (n.p., 2016).

37. Theodore Schleifer, "Ted Cruz Endorses Donald Trump," *CNN Politics* (September 23, 2016).

38. Christopher Ingraham, "About 100 Million People Couldn't Be Bothered to Vote This Year," *Washington Post* (November 12, 2016). "Other" included the candidates of the Libertarian and Green Parties, who together garnered over six million votes.

39. Michael Barbaro, "Americans Don't Trust Her. But Why?" *New York Times* (August 16, 2016).

40. Alex Seitz-Wald, "Hillary Clinton Struggles to Explain $600K in Goldman Sachs Speaking Fees," NBC News (February 4, 2016).

41. https://www.youtube.com/watch?v=DkS9y5t0tR0, accessed September 10, 2018.

42. Tim Hains, "Hillary Clinton: Voting for Iraq War Was, 'From My Perspective, My Mistake,'" *RealClear Politics* (September 7, 2016).

43. https://www.youtube.com/watch?v=Fgcd1ghag5Y, accessed September 10, 2018.

44. "Full Transcript: Democratic Presidential Debate," *New York Times* (October 4, 2015).

45. https://wikileaks.org/clinton-emails/, accessed September 10, 2018.

46. Clinton, *What Happened*, 236.

47. Office of Hillary Rodham Clinton, "Hillary's Vision for America," https://www.hillaryclinton.com/issues/, accessed September 11, 2018.

48. David Jackson, "Donald Trump Accepts GOP Nomination, Says 'I Alone Can Fix' System," *USA Today* (July 21, 2016).

49. "Money Raised as of December 31," *Washington Post*, https://www.washingtonpost.com/graphics/politics/2016-election/campaign-finance/, accessed September 11, 2018; Alan Yuhas, "Trump Campaign Doubles Spending but Staff Is a Tenth the Size of Clinton's," *Guardian* (August 21, 2016); John Hudson, "Inside Hillary Clinton's Massive Foreign-Policy Brain Trust," *Foreign Policy* (February 10, 2016); "Read Hillary Clinton's 'Basket of Deplorables' Remarks About Donald Trump Supporters," *Time* (September 10, 2016).

50. Tom Engelhardt, "Has the American Age of Decline Begun?," *TomDispatch* (April 26, 2016).

8. ATTENDING TO RABBIT'S QUESTION

1. Thomas L. Friedman, "Homeless in America," *New York Times* (November 8, 2016).

2. Maureen Dowd, "Absorbing the Impossible," *New York Times* (November 9, 2016).

3. Gail Collins, "Ten-Step Program for Adjusting to President-Elect Trump," *New York Times* (November 9, 2016).

4. Frank Bruni, "Trump's Shocking Success," *New York Times* (November 9, 2016).

5. Roger Cohen, "President Donald Trump," *New York Times* (November 9, 2016).

6. Charles M. Blow, "America Elects a Bigot," *New York Times* (November 10, 2016).

7. David Brooks, "The View from Trump Tower," *New York Times* (November 11, 2016).

8. Paul Krugman, "Thoughts for the Horrified," *New York Times* (November 11, 2016).

9. Ross Douthat, "You Must Serve Trump," *New York Times* (November 11, 2016).

10. Charles Blow's columns for the *New York Times* are archived at https://www.nytimes.com/column/charles-m-blow, accessed September 12, 2018.

11. Carl Bernstein, "Trump Presidency Is Worse Than Watergate," *RealClear Politics* (August 3, 2018).

12. Olivia Gordon, "Trump Is No Hitler—He's a Mussolini, Says Oxford Historian," *Oxford Today* (April 24, 2017); Jed Gottlieb, "Trump Is America's Franco: How Fascism Finds a Foothold in Democratic Nations," *Paste* (October 11, 2016); A. Dirk Moses, Federico Finchelstein, and Pablo Piccato, "Juan Perón Shows How Trump Could Destroy Our Democracy Without Tearing It Down," *Washington Post* (March 22, 2017); Michael Cohen, "Trump the Traitor," *Boston Globe* (July 16, 2018).

13. Eliza Collins, "Les Moonves: Trump's Run Is 'Damn Good for CBS,'" *Politico* (February 29, 2016).

14. Hannity of *Fox News*, Cooper of CNN, and Maddow of MSNBC, respectively.

15. Henry Porter, "Witnessing History in Chicago's Grant Park," *Vanity Fair* (November 2018).

16. Ben Smith, "Obama on Small-Town Pa.: Clinging to Religion, Guns, Xenophobia," *Politico* (April 11, 2008).

17. Abraham Lincoln, "First Inaugural Address" (March 4, 1861).

18. George W. Bush, "State of the Union Address" (January 29, 2002).

19. For a near-contemporaneous assessment, see Seymour M. Hersh, "Torture at Abu Ghraib," *New Yorker* (May 10, 2004).

20. Sarah Anderson, "The Postal Worker's Christmas," *New York Times* (December 18, 2018).

21. Norman Mailer, "An Evening with Jackie Kennedy," *Esquire* (July 1962).

22. "I Am Part of the Resistance Inside the Trump Administration," *New York Times* (September 5, 2018).

23. David Welna, "Trump Has Vowed to Fill Guantanamo with 'Some Bad Dudes'—But Who?," NPR (November 14, 2016).

24. Heather Long, "Under Trump's Watch, the U.S. Is on Track for the Highest Trade Deficit in 10 Years," *Washington Post* (August 3, 2018).

25. TreasuryDirect, "Historical Debt Outstanding, Annual 2000–2017," https://www.treasurydirect.gov/govt/reports/pd/histdebt/histdebt _histo5.htm, accessed September 24, 2018.

26. International Atomic Energy Agency, "IAEA Director General's Introductory Statement to the Board of Governors" (September 10, 2018).

27. Liudas Dapkas, "Lithuania Signs Agreement with U.S. on Troop Deployment," *Military Times* (January 17, 2017).

28. Sam Meredith, "Trump Says NATO Withdrawal Is 'Unnecessary' After Allies Agree to Increase Spending," CNBC (July 12, 2018).

29. Nick Turse, "A Wider World of War," *TomDispatch* (December 14, 2017).

30. Leo Shane III, "Trump Changes His Mind Again on Military Spending, Now Wants a Big Boost Next Year," *Military Times* (December 10, 2018).

31. Sandra Erwin, "Trump: 'We Are Going to Have the Space Force,'" *Space News* (June 18, 2018).

32. Julia Edwards Ainsley, "Trump Border 'Wall' to Cost $21.6 Billion, Take 3.5 Years to Build: Internal Report," Reuters (February 9, 2017).

33. "Key Quotes from Reuters Interview with Trump," Reuters (August 20, 2018).

34. David Nakamura and Abby Phillip, "Trump Announces New Strategy for Afghanistan That Calls for a Troop Increase," *Washington Post* (August 21, 2017).

35. Environmental Defense Fund, "How Climate Change Plunders the Planet," https://www.edf.org/climate/how-climate-change-plunders-planet, accessed September 27, 2018.

36. Tara Copp, "Pentagon Is Still Preparing for Global Warming Even Though Trump Said to Stop," *Military Times* (September 12, 2017).

37. "A Greener Bush," *Economist* (February 13, 2003).

38. Nick Turse, "Victory in Our Time," *TomDispatch* (September 4, 2018). The quotation is from Tom Engelhardt's introduction to Turse's essay.

39. *The Writings and Speeches of Edmund Burke*, Paul Langford, ed. (Oxford, 1997), vol. 1, 137–138.

ACKNOWLEDGMENTS

With the advent of old age comes an acute awareness of how swiftly the sand trickles through the neck of the hourglass. Does that neck widen with the passage of time? It seems to.

Yet with age also comes greater appreciation for kindnesses received along the way. I am the recipient of many blessings, none of them earned. Not least among them are the love of my family and the benevolence (and tolerance) of friends. The dedication of this book records my immeasurable gratitude for one such friend, who held out his hand at a moment when I was most in need. Eliot Cohen's generosity back when the post–Cold War era was just getting underway made all the difference.

As for this particular project, other friends and acquaintances helped in ways large and small. They include Lawrence Kaplan, Cathy Lutz, Roy Scranton, Wick Sloane, and David Warsh. An early morning breakfast at Cornell University with Professor Peter Katzenstein was particularly useful in helping me translate an inkling into a potential book.

The resourceful staff of the Walpole Public Library responded to my various requests quickly and efficiently. A special note of thanks to Richard Fomo for the author photo and to Reggie Goehring for her pointed assistance as things were drawing to a close.

At Metropolitan Books, I am grateful to Sara Bershtel and her wonderful team. It is a privilege to be associated with such a professional organization. As for my agent John Wright and my editor Tom Engelhardt, I've said it before: They are the best in the business—and invaluable friends as well.

Andrew Bacevich
Walpole, Massachusetts
April 2019

INDEX

ABOUT THE AUTHOR

ANDREW BACEVICH is professor emeritus of history and international relations at Boston University and president of the Quincy Institute for Responsible Statecraft. A graduate of both the U.S. Military Academy and Princeton University, he served in the U.S. Army for twenty-three years. His recent books include *Breach of Trust*, *The Limits of Power*, *America's War for the Greater Middle East*, and *Twilight of the American Century*. His writings have appeared in the *New York Times*, the *London Review of Books*, and the *American Conservative*, among other publications.